THE SMALL BUSINESS PROGRAMME HANDBOOK

THE SMALL BUSINESS PROGRAMME HANDBOOK

Information to help the growing business

P·C·P
Paul Chapman
Publishing Ltd

THE SMALL BUSINESS PROGRAMME

This edition first published 1990
Paul Chapman Publishing Ltd
144 Liverpool Road
London N1 1LA

British Library Cataloguing in Publication Data

The small business programme handbook
1. Small firms. Management
I. Cranfield School of Management
658.022

ISBN 1 85396 125 6

Typeset by Burns & Smith Ltd., Derby
Printed and bound by Butler & Tanner, Frome, Somerset

CONTENTS

The Small Business Programme

The Small Business Programme is designed to help your business grow and to control that growth. It is based on twenty-five independent modules, in vital areas of interest to your business. Each module typically comprises a video tape, an audio tape and a workbook, which integrate to become a comprehensive business development programme supported by a locally organized workshop.

The Small Business Programme has been developed by experts from Cranfield School of Management and the Open University to be suitable for the needs of your business. You select the modules to suit your business circumstances. The Programme helps you develop your management expertise. It then helps you apply the techniques you learn to the problems your business faces, in a structured, systematic way. It shows you how other small firms do this so that you can build upon their experience.

Each module is:

1. *Friendly, informative and entertaining* The video and audio tapes have been produced by the BBC. They use a 'magazine format' with professional presenters introducing graphics, case histories, experts and well-known entrepreneurs in a way that is designed to bring the topic alive. The workbooks are also attractively produced and easy to use with simple step-by-step checklists, activities and many standard business forms.
2. *Problem based* Many years of research indicate that growing firms face similar problems. The workbooks are structured around activities that address these problems. They allow you to apply management techniques to your firm in a structured way. It is like having a course designed with just your business in mind.
3. *Full of examples* Hundreds of successful and not so successful small firms have opened the door on the problems they face and show how they overcome them by applying management techniques. You gain from their experience.

This easy-to-use format gives you:

1. *Flexibility* You complete the module *when and where* you want. You can work at your home or your office, at any time of the day or night. The audio tape is designed to be played in the car, so that you can use the time you waste in traffic jams to good advantage. The workbook is broken down into sections so that you can pick it up and put it down when it suits you.
2. *Convenience* You complete the module *at your own pace*. You do not have to comply with the strict timetable of formal learning. And you can use it again and again when you need it.
3. *Privacy* You apply the management techniques to the problems of your business *with complete confidentiality*. The Programme shows you how to do this in a systematic, structured way. You do not have to tell others about the problems or opportunities your business faces.

If you want, there are locally organized workshops to help you with the Programme. The workshops introduce you to consultants who will help you with the material. They also allow you to meet other owner-managers of local firms. They are structured in such a way as to explain and amplify some of the more complex concepts but allow sufficient time to discuss the practical problems of applying them.

With all these elements, the Small Business Programme builds into a comprehensive business development package which helps you develop your management skills and unlock the true potential of your firm.

The Small Business Programme
Cranfield School of Management
Cranfield
Bedford MK43 0AL
Tel: 0234 750414/751122

The Small Business Programme Modules

The Small Business programme is based on twenty-five independent modules that integrate to become a comprehensive business development programme. Each module generally comprises a video tape, an audio tape and a workbook and is accompanied by a workshop.

AC1	**Managing the Growing Business: An Introduction to the Small Business Programme**

M1	**Marketing**	A1	**Accounting**
M2	Developing Products and Services	A2	Financial Decisions
M3	Using Design	A3	Budgeting
M4	Pricing	A4	Book-keeping and Accounting Systems
M5	Advertising and Promotion	A5	Taxation
M6	Selling	A6	Debtor Control
		A7	Stock Control
P1	**People: Managing the Organisation**		
P2	Selecting Employees	F1	Premises
P3	Time Management	F2	Office Management
P4	Leadership	F3	Using Computers
AP1	The Business Plan	S1	Retailing
AP2	Financing Growth	S2	Production Management

Preface

Knowledge itself is power

Francis Bacon

Many people dream of starting their own business and getting it to grow, but few actually do so. Running your own business is not a simple task. You have to be a jack-of-all-trades, willing to lend a hand with all aspects of the business when necessary, yet also keep overall control and give the firm the direction it needs. You must be willing to take the measured risks that other people seek to avoid. More than anything, you need to have stamina, courage and sheer determination to make your business succeed.

Anything that can make the task easier is welcomed. And, in today's rapidly changing market-place, one of the greatest needs any business has is for information. Information is the bedrock on which sound business decisions are made. The problem is that information comes in different ways: from individuals, from books, from magazines, from reference manuals, from computers, from trade fairs...from a whole range of different sources. What is more, this information is located in hundreds of different places. The key questions for any businessman are therefore:

1. What information is available?
2. Where can I find it?

This Handbook answers these questions. It tells you what information is available, in seven key areas:

1. Sources of help and advice.
2. Sources of market information.

3. Financial and other business assistance.
4. Training.
5. Obtaining finance.
6. Exporting and importing.
7. Business and the law.

Time spent in planning and preparation is rarely wasted. And information is the key to effective planning. This Handbook is an invaluable source of information for the growing firm. Without it you could waste many hours trying to find the information you need.

Acknowledgements

Text compiled by Colin Barrow, Paul Burns, and Jean Harrison.
Supervising Editor: Paul Burns
Cartoons: Gary Rees

1 Sources of Help and Advice

There are hundreds of organizations that provide free or subsidized help and advice for smaller firms. They can advise you on aspects of marketing, accounting, law or tax; they can help you to find finance, premises or personnel. Locally based organizations can also introduce you to other small firms where you might find new customers or suppliers. Good advice can save you time and money. It can help you to make the right decisions and avoid the pitfalls of others.

If you have a simple query, you might be able to obtain the answer by telephone; a more complicated one might involve a personal visit or a visit by the adviser to your premises. Finding the right adviser has a great deal to do with personal chemistry, so it is often worthwhile trying more than one of the organizations listed in this chapter. However, if an organization you contact cannot help you, it should be able to put you in touch with one that can.

It is worth remembering, however, that if your query involves an element of business judgement, even experts might differ in their recommendations. So it is particularly worthwhile seeking a range of opinions. At the end of the day the responsibility for any decision is yours, not your adviser's.

These organizations can provide general and often comprehensive help and advice to small and growing businesses. Other organizations listed elsewhere in this Handbook can also assist, but if they are principally providers of grants, financial help or highly specialized assistance they are described in the appropriate section. This is particularly true of those organizations and initiatives listed in Chapter 3. If the advisers listed here cannot help, remember your accountant and solicitor. You may also decide to approach a management consultant.

Why seek help and advice?

Pros

- Free or subsidized advice
- You gain from the experience of others
- You save time and money
- You develop confidence in your final decision

Cons

- You spend a lot of time finding an appropriate adviser
- You can be given bad advice, particularly where judgement is involved
- The responsibility for any decision still rests with you

A. ENTERPRISE AGENCIES

Some 300 local enterprise agencies are now operated throughout the UK. The vast majority are co-ordinated under the umbrella of Business in the Community (BIC), a charity formed by a consortium of big business, to help foster the enterprise culture.

These agencies are usually run by a small staff, for the most part secondees from BIC's sponsors, and they can help advise across a broad spectrum of business matters. Where they don't themselves have the answer they will undoubtedly 'know a man who does', to borrow the AA's slogan. Their services are free and they should be your first port of call for help with such matters as employment law, VAT, advertising, finding local premises, market research, bookkeeping, raising finance and exporting.

Two services of particular value to the owner–manager are the local business club, often co-ordinated by or based on an enterprise agency, where people can meet others facing similar problems; and the 'marriage bureau', which can put you in touch with people who either have or require resources to help with expansion.

You can obtain the address of your local enterprise agency from your telephone directory or from BIC:

Business in the Community
227a City Road
London EC1V 1LX
Tel: 01 253 3716

B. GOVERNMENT HELP

The Small Firms Service

The Small Firms Service is provided by the Department of Employment through a nationwide network of thirteen centres and over 200 area counselling offices throughout Great Britain.

The Service can help existing or potential small businesses with almost any type of business inquiry. It can advise on raising finance, government grants, patents, VAT, sources of supply, industrial training, exporting, taxation, personnel development and management, marketing, market research and new technology. The Service provides an extensive network of useful contacts in local and national government, chambers of commerce and the professions, for example, who can help solve most business problems.

A Small Firms Service information adviser is the first port of call. If information or contacts are required he or she can usually deal with the inquiry on the spot, using the Service's computerised database. Alternatively, he or she can arrange for a meeting with a business counsellor, an experienced business person who can offer impartial and confidential advice and guidance. If, after meeting a counsellor, you need highly specialized advice, arrangements can usually be made for an appointment with an appropriate consultant. Meetings with counsellors can be either at a local area counselling office or at the client's own premises. The information service is free as are the first three counselling sessions. Thereafter, a modest charge is made.

To contact your regional Small Firms Centre dial 100 and ask for Freefone Enterprise, or you can telephone direct - or just walk in. The offices are listed below.

Small Firms Centres

Birmingham
9th Floor, Alpha Tower
Suffolk Street
Queensway
Birmingham B1 1TT
Tel: Freefone Enterprise

Bristol
6th Floor, The Pithay
Bristol BS1 2NB
Tel: Freefone Enterprise

Cambridge
Carlyle House
Carlyle Road
Cambridge CB4 3DN
Tel: Freefone Enterprise

Cardiff
16 St David's House
Wood Street
Cardiff CF1 1ER
Tel: Freefone Enterprise

Glasgow
120 Bothwell Street
Glasgow G2 6NR
Tel: Freefone Enterprise

Leeds
1 Park Row
City Square
Leeds LS1 5NR
Tel: Freefone Enterprise

Liverpool
Graeme House
Derby Square
Liverpool L2 7UJ
Tel: Freefone Enterprise

London
2nd Floor
11 Belgrave Road
London SW1V 1RB
Tel: Freefone Enterprise

Manchester
26/28 Deansgate
Manchester M3 1RH
Tel: Freefone Enterprise

Newcastle
15th Floor, Cale Cross House
156 Pilgrim Street
Newcastle upon Tyne NE1 6PZ
Tel: Freefone Enterprise

Nottingham
57 Maid Marian Way
Nottingham NG1 6GE
Tel: Freefone Enterprise

Reading
Abbey Hall
Abbey Square
Reading RG1 3BE
Tel: Freefone Enterprise

Stevenage
Business & Technology Centre
Bessemer Drive
Stevenage
Hert SG1 2DX
Tel: Freefone Enterprise

In Northern Ireland the Local Enterprise Development Unit offers a similar service. See Chapter 3, Section B: Regional assistance for further information and contact points.

C. OTHER ORGANIZATIONS

The Rural Development Commission Business Service

The Rural Development Commission was created in 1988 by bringing together into a single organization the long-established Development Commission and its small business agency, the Council for Small Industries in Rural Areas (CoSIRA). The Commission's Business Service now provides the services previously provided by CoSIRA.

The Business Service is based at thirty-one offices all over rural England. It provides business and technical advice and skill training to firms with fewer than twenty employees in areas with under 10,000 inhabitants. Outside England, similar services are on offer from Mid Wales Development, the Scottish Developoment Agency, the Highlands and Islands Development Board and in Northern Ireland by the Local Enterprise Development Unit - all listed and described in Chapter 3.

In summary the Business Service covers the following areas.

Technical and professional advice

The business adviser can arrange for a technical or professional adviser to give specialist help with difficult problems. The Commission's team of professional and technical advisers have all worked in industry and have a wide range of skills and experience, outlined below. Advice is normally given on a working visit to the client's factory or workshop.

Business management advice

1. Accountancy, bookkeeping, profit planning, cash flow forecasting, costing, applications for loans and overdraft facilities.
2. Marketing, market research, product planning, pricing and distribution, advertising and sales, export, exhibitions.
3. Production management, planning and control of production, buying and stock control, staff recruitment, employment legislation, statutory sick pay, supervisor training, use of microcomputers.

Technical advice

1. Building and estimating, structural engineering, joinery, building conversions, thatching, dry stone walling.
2. Mechanical engineering, electrical engineering, industrial safety, welding techniques, Computer Numerically Controlled machine tools, low-cost

automation, jig and tool design, workshop layout, fibre-glass lamination, thermoplastics, clay products technology and pottery, abrasive wheels, vehicle electrics.

3. Furniture making, antique furniture restoration, upholstery, woodworking machinery, spraying and finishing, wheelwrighting.
4. Sawmill management, timber technology, saw doctoring.
5. Farriery, forgework.
6. Saddlery and leatherwork.
7. Engineering products and prototypes: the Commission's own workshops can undertake the design and production of jigs, press tools and special-purpose machinery for small firms. They will also develop prototypes. This service is particularly valuable to non-engineering businesses.

Finance

The Commission normally expects the major part of funding for small businesses to be arranged with a bank or other commercial lending source. However, it has its own limited loan fund which can be used in appropriate cases to finance part of the cost of the project, up to a maximum of £75,000. The repayment period may be between two and twenty years according to the type of loan. Management accountants are available to assist with the preparation of a case to support an application for a loan.

The Commission has agreements with major banks which provide favourable terms for client businesses and opportunities for joint lending by the Commission and the bank.

Grants

Grants are not generally available for rural businesses; however, in certain circumstances the Commission does make grants to help a business start up or expand.

In 1984 the Commission established its priority areas (called Rural Development Areas) following a review using criteria set by government. These are considered to be the parts of rural England in greatest need of assistance and it is here that the Commission concentrates the greatest part of its resources. There are twenty-eight Rural Development Areas in the remoter parts of England, covering generally the North, the East Coast, the Welsh borders and the West Country.

In Rural Development Areas only, grants are available towards the cost of converting unused and redundant buildings into workshops, or into certain types of tourist facility, including the cost of installing or upgrading mains services.

In all areas grants may be available to help with the cost of taking a stand at a trade show or exhibition, or the cost of engaging a consultant to draft a marketing plan for your product.

Assistance may be available from the Rural Transport Development Fund if you are starting a new bus service in a rural area.

Training

If a client's owner or employees need training or an extra skill, perhaps how to weld stainless steel, repair electronic ignition on a car, upholster an antique chair, or increase production from a spindle moulder, the business adviser can help. He can arrange either a visit from a technical adviser or one of the Commission's intensive two-to-five day courses, which are planned to give practical skills with a minimum waste of working time.

New Entrant Training Scheme (NETS)

The Rural Development Commission provides longer periods of training for a limited number of young people, usually under nineteen years of age. They must already be employed by a business employing less than twenty people in an eligible area. The training provided consists of a series of one-week sessions over a period of from one to three years. NETS training is available in most of the skills mentioned earlier.

Other services

Village shops

Advice is given on the purchase and management of a village shop. Residential weekend courses on 'Buying a Village Shop' and 'Professional Management for Small Shopkeepers' are arranged at a number of centres.

Sales promotion

The Commission arranges group stands at a series of national trade fairs and exhibitions on which clients can exhibit their products at much lower costs than on an independent stand. Regular marketing seminars are arranged all over England that can help with all aspects of advertising, promotion and selling service.

Rural transport

The Commission's transport advisers can help with licensing, new laws and regulations, sources of financial assistance, route planning and registration, whether clients operate or plan to operate hire cars, taxis, or buses serving country areas.

Tourism

In Rural Development Areas the Commission gives assistance to tourist and leisure enterprises, guest houses, bed-and-breakfasts and small hotels, as well as to restaurants, activity centres and tourist attractions. In addition to other financial and professional help, tourist advisers - with wide experience of the trade - can help you to start up or expand your business.

Offices of the Commission

Head Office
11 Cowley Street
London SW1P 3NA
Tel: 01 276 6969

or

141 Castle Street
Salisbury
Wiltshire SP1 3TP
Tel: 0722 336255

North Region

Rural Development Commission
Business Service
Northern Regional Office
Ullswater Road, Penrith,
Cumbria CA11 7EH.
Tel: 0768 67294

Rural Development Commission
Business Service
12 Churchfield Court
Barnsley, South Yorkshire S70 2JT.
Tel: 0226 204367

Rural Development Commission
Business Service
Morton Road,
Yarm Road Industrial Estate
Darlington, Co. Durham DL1 4PT.
Tel: 0325 487123

Rural Development Commission
Business Service
Leachfield Estate
Green Lane West
Garstang
Lancs PR3 1NJ
Tel: 09952 4117

Rural Development Commission
Business Service
14 Market Place, Howden
Goole, North Humberside DN14 7BJ.
Tel: 0430 431138

Rural Development Commission
Business Service
Northumberland Business Centre
Southgate, Morpeth
Northumberland NE61 2EH.
Tel: 0670 511221

Rural Development Commission
Business Service
Ullswater Road, Penrith,
Cumbria CA11 7EH.
Tel: 0768 65752

Rural Development Commission
Business Service
William House, Shipton Road,
Skelton
York YO3 6XW.
Tel: 0904 646866

West Region

Rural Development Commission
Business Service
Western Regional Office
Strickland House, The Lawns
Park Street, Wellington, Telford
Shropshire TF1 3BX.
Tel: 0952 57400

Rural Development Commission
Business Service
6 Shropshire Street
Audlem, Cheshire CW3 0DY
Tel: 0270 812012

Rural Development Commission
Business Service
Stanley House, 47a High Street
Henley in Arden, Solihull
West Midlands B95 5AA.
Tel: 05642 4191

Rural Development Commission
Business Service
32 Church Street, Malvern
Worcs. WR14 2AZ.
Tel: 06845 64784 or 64506

Rural Development Commission
Business Service
Strickland House, The Lawns
Park Street, Wellington, Telford
Shropshire TF1 3BX
Tel: 0952 47161

Rural Development Commission
Business Service
Ravenstor Road, Wirksworth
Derbyshire DE4 4FY
Tel: 062982 4848

East Region

Rural Development Commission
Business Service
Eastern Regional Office
Chancel House, East Street
Bingham, Notts NG13 8DR.
Tel: 0949 37268

Rural Development Commission
Business Service
Chancel House, East Street
Bingham, Notts NG13 8DR.
Tel: 0949 39222

Rural Development Commission
Business Service
24 Brooklands Avenue
Cambridge CB2 2BU.
Tel: 0223 354505

Rural Development Commission
Business Service
133 High Street, Hadleigh
Ipswich, Suffolk IP7 5EJ.
Tel: 0473 827893

Rural Development Commission
Business Service
Hunsbury Hill Centre, Harksome Hill
Northampton NN4 9QX.
Tel: 0604 765874

Rural Development Commission
Business Service
13 Unthank Road, Norwich
Norfolk NR2 2PA.
Tel: 0603 624498

Rural Development Commission
Business Service
Council Offices, Eastgate
Sleaford, Lincs NG34 7EB.
Tel: 0529 414144

South West Region

Rural Development Commission
Business Service
South Western Regional Office
27 Victoria Park Road, Exeter
Devon EX2 4NT.
Tel: 0392 215447

Rural Development Commission
Business Service
141 Castle Street, Salisbury
Wiltshire SP1 3TP.
Tel: 0722 336255

Rural Development Commission
Business Service
209 Redland Road, Bristol BS6 6YU.
Tel: 0272 733433.

Rural Development Commission
Business Service
Wing D, Government Buildings
Prince of Wales Road
Dorchester, Dorset DT1 1QJ.
Tel: 0305 268558

Rural Development Commission
Business Service
27 Victoria Park Road, Exeter, Devon EX2 4NT.
Tel: 0392 52616

Rural Development Commission
Business Service
3 Charfield House
Castle Street
Taunton
Somerset
Tel: 0823 276905

Rural Development Commission
Business Service
2nd Floor, Highshore House
New Bridge Street, Truro
Cornwall TR1 2AA.
Tel: 0872 73531

South East Region

Rural Development Commission
Business Service
South Eastern Regional Office
141 Castle Street, Salisbury, Wiltshire SP1 3TP
Tel: 0722 3365255

Rural Development Commission
Business Service
Agriculture House
55 Goldington Road,
Bedford MK40 3LU.
Tel: 0234 261381

Rural Development Commission
Business Service
64a High Street, Braintree,
Essex CM7 7JP.
Tel: 0376 47623

Rural Development Commission
Business Service
6/7 Town Lane, Newport
Isle of Wight PO30 1JU.
Tel: 0983 528019

Rural Development Commission
Business Service
8 Romney Place, Maidstone
Kent ME15 6LE.
Tel: 0622 765222

Rural Development Commission
Business Service
Sussex House, 212 High Street
Lewes, Sussex BN7 2NH.
Tel: 0273 471399

Rural Development Commission
Business Service
The Maltings
St John's Road, Wallingford
Oxon. OX10 9BZ.
Tel: 0491 35523

Rural Development Commission
Business Service
Barton Farm
Andover Road, Winchester
Hampshire SO22 6AX.
Tel: 0962 880503

The Co-operative Development Agency (CDA)

The CDA was established by Parliament in 1978 with all-party support to promote the concept of co-operatives. It is funded and supervised by the Small Firms Service and is scheduled to operate until at least mid-1990. It gives advice on the mechanics and philosophy of industrial co-operatives to people starting up in business, or wishing to convert an existing business into a co-operative.

The CDA can also help with the appraisal of specific projects, including assessing products, markets, available skills, finance and the prospects of success. Advice may be obtained on legal, taxation and publicity matters; sources of finance; and under recently extended powers the CDA acts as a provider of training.

Where users are able to pay, the CDA charges the costs of providing advice and assistance.

For further information contact:

The Co-operative Development
Agency
Broadmead House
21 Panton Street
London SW1Y 4DR
Tel: 01 839 2987

Alliance of Small Firms and Self-Employed People

The Alliance aims to represent and publicize the interests of its members at both national and local level. Membership is by annual subscription, and a legal expenses insurance cover is available for a further payment. Members can use the Alliance's inquiry services, which gives advice and information on a wide range of tax, legal and employment matters. If it cannot give you an answer it will put you in touch with a consultant who can. The first consultation is free, and thereafter you agree a price with the consultant direct.

For further information contact the Alliance at:

Alliance of Small Firms and Self-Employed People
33 The Green
Calne
Wilts SN11 8DJ
Tel: 0249 817003

Association of Independent Businesses

The Association was established in 1968 to promote the cause of the smaller business. Its aim is to remove discrimination against independent businesses in existing and proposed legislation, and it therefore maintains close contact with both Whitehall and Westminister. Its small national office staff have a limited capacity to answer members' queries on typical problems that face independent businesses. They can also signpost inquirers to other useful sources of advice.

For further information contact the Association at:

Association of Independent Businesses
133 Copeland Road
London SE15 3SP
Tel: 01 277 5158/5097

Forum of Private Business

The Forum is a non-profit-making organization with the objectives of promoting and preserving a system of free competitive enterprise in the UK, and also of giving private people a greater say in the legislation that affects their business. The Forum researches and distributes a referendum nine times a year, keeping members informed and seeking their views on a number of topical and important business issues. It makes government aware of these views both directly and by various public relations activities. The Forum also plays a role by initiating training programmes in schools and colleges to show the importance of free enterprise in our society.

For further information contact the Forum at:

Forum of Private Business
Ruskin Chambers
Drury Lane
Knutsford
Cheshire WA16 6HA
Tel: 0565 4467

Institute of Directors

The Institute represents the interests both of the directors of large companies and owner–directors of smaller ones. In particular, it has a service for putting those looking for funds or other resources in touch with those with funds to invest.

For further information contact the Institute at:

Institute of Directors
116 Pall Mall
London SW1Y 5ED
Tel: 01 839 1233

National Federation of Self-Employed and Small Businesses

The Federation is a campaigning pressure group in business to promote and protect the interests of all who are either self-employed or who own or are directors of small businesses. Formed in 1974, it now has some 50,000 members in 300 branches throughout the UK. The Federation has the funds to take major test cases of importance to small business through the expensive legal process leading to the House of Lords or European Court of Human Rights. It has been particularly effective in taxation and VAT matters.

Among other benefits, members are covered by a legal expenses compensation cover scheme. The cover includes:

(a) VAT tribunal representation and costs up to £10,000 per case to appeal in VAT disputes;
(b) defence of health and safety prosecutions, covering costs of prosecution under the Health and Safety at Work Act 1974;
(c) in-depth investigation cover to meet accountants' fees in helping to deal with an Inland Revenue investigation;
(d) industrial tribunal compensation awards to meet unfair dismissal awards (this is supported by a telephone legal advice service).

There is a joining fee, and full membership is by annual subscriptions.

For further information contact the Federation at:

National Federation of Self-Employed and Small Businesses
32 St Annes Road,
Lytham St Annes
Lancashire FY8 1NY
Tel: 0253 720911

Press and Parliamentary Office
140 Lower Marsh
Westminster Bridge
London SE1 7AE
Tel: 01 928 9272

The Small Business Bureau

Formed in 1976, the Bureau aims to serve the needs of the small business community. Membership is by annual subscription and gives you access to its advisory service and a copy of its monthly newspaper, *Small Business*. It also represents the small business point of view to government, organizes trade delegations and provides European opportunities through its involvement with EMSU (the European Medium and Small Business Union).

For further information contact the Bureau at:

The Small Business Bureau
32 Smith Square
London SW1P 3HH
Tel: 01 222 0330

Trade associations

Most business fields have a trade association, such as the Brewers Society, the Federation of Fish Friers, or the Booksellers Association. They are a useful source of help and advice to potential new entrants to their trade. The *Directory of British Associations* lists all such associations.

Details can be obtained from:

Directory of British Associations
CBD Research Ltd
Chancery House
Wickam Road
Beckenham
Kent BR3 2JS
Tel: 01 650 7745

Chambers of commerce

Local chambers of commerce vary greatly in the level of help and advice they provide. Some are no more than informal 'clubs' of local business persons; others provide fully fledged business information services. Apart from playing an important role in providing information and help for existing businesses, chambers of commerce have been a major force in the launch of many of the most prominent and effective enterprise agencies.

They have also sponsored many local new business competitions. They are a very important source of information, advice and help for new and small businesses.

You can obtain the address of your local chamber either from Yellow Pages or:

Association of British Chambers of Commerce
Sovereign House
212 Shaftesbury Avenue
London WC2H 8EW
Tel: 01 240 5831/6

D. PROFESSIONAL ADVICE

Accountants

The only accountants legally allowed to audit company accounts are members of the four institutes listed below. All institutes keep lists of members and they can put you in touch with firms practising in your area:

Institute of Chartered Accountants in England and Wales
Chartered Accountants Hall
PO Box 433
Moorgate Place
London EC2P 2BJ
Tel: 01 628 7060

Institute of Chartered Accountants in Scotland
27 Queen Street
Edinburgh EH2 1LA
Tel: 031 225 5673

Institute of Chartered Accountants in Ireland
Chartered Accountants House
87–89 Pembroke Road
Dublin 4
Tel: 0001 680 400

Chartered Association of Certified Accountants
29 Lincoln's Inn Fields
London WC2A 3EE
Tel: 01 242 6855

However, the following organizations may be useful if you wish to recruit an accountant to work in your firm. Members of the Society of Company and Commercial Accountants specialize in providing accounting services for small firms.

Chartered Institute of Management Accountants
63 Portland Place
London W1N 4AB
Tel: 01 637 2311

Society of Company and Commercial Accountants
40 Tyndalls Park Road
Bristol BS8 1PL
Tel: 0272 738261

Solicitors

The Law Society will provide you with names of firms of solicitors in your area. It also publishes booklets giving details of solicitors willing to undertake legal aid work.

Its address is:

The Law Society
113 Chancery Lane
London WC2A 1PL
Tel: 01 242 1222

E. ADVICE ON COMPUTERS

As computers come down in price, more and more firms are using them. However, a computer can be either a time-saving tool or a time-consuming distraction, and you need to think carefully about whether your firm really needs one yet. Of course, the computer is excellent for dealing with repetitive clerical and analytical tasks and repetitive reporting or information searches. The key is the degree of data repetition which must be handled.

In a competitive environment the speed of response to meet customers' requirements, or provide information, is increasingly vital to winning and retaining business. But this must be balanced against the cost of a computer-based solution to the problem. You need to buy the hardware (the computer and the related equipment), the software (the programs to run on the computer) and train your staff to use the system. You must realize that you are unlikely to reduce your staff by instaling a computer. Instead, you will find that your service levels improve and you produce more, and better, information.

A microcomputer will suit the needs of most small firms at a cost ranging from a few hundred pounds to up to £10,000. The softwards costs will probably be higher. Part of the reason for that is the temptation to buy 'add-on' packages so that your system does everything from word processing and data handling to accounting or stock control. However, it is sensible to think about your complete information needs and to make sure that you buy a computer that can handle all the functions you want now and in the near future.

The amount of money you spend on hardware depends upon the type of equipment purchased but, more important, upon the storage capacity you need. Information is stored both in the computer and on magnetic disks. The more information you store, the more expensive the computer system. Your storage requirement is largely dictated by the functions you require the computer to perform and the volume of transactions it will handle. Make sure the system you select has adequate storage to run the software you select and deal with the volume of transactions that faces your business now and over, say, the next two years. A second consideration is the speed of access of the information stored. The quicker the access time, generally the more expensive the equipment.

Most small companies buy proprietary software packages. These can be adapted in some small ways to meet the particular requirements of the company. But, by and large, the company must adapt to the system, not the other way around. There are many proprietary systems on the market: for bookkeeping, management accounting, payroll, mailing and price lists and also word processing. The best are the 'integrated business systems', which offer many functions: for example, accounting systems along with stock control systems that allow you to monitor physical stock levels, credit control systems designed to speed up payments from your debtors, budgetary systems which allow you to compare actual results to budgets, or job costing systems which integrate with the nominal ledger.

These systems also enable you to take data from the accounting systems and store it separately for use with other programs such as word processing or spreadsheets. For example, you might develop a mailing list from your sales/debtor ledger to which you send a standard word-processed letter. Similarly, you may work on accounting data using a spreadsheet programmed to develop your budgets, quite separate from your accounting system. Most systems are 'modular' so that different processes in the system can be run separately. However, they are also 'integrated', which means that one module can pass information to another.

Packages exist for many industries and professions including shopkeepers, solicitors, medical practices and estate agents. Your trade association will help you find out more. It always pays to shop around.

As your business grows, you will eventually need to purchase a computer and computer-based systems. Buy a reputable package from a reputable dealer. Try to see it in operation before you purchase and ensure that the dealer will provide you with advice and back-up if things go wrong. A properly working 'integrated business system' will help you control your company as it grows. It will give you the information you need, when you need it. After a while you will wonder how you coped without it.

Should I use a computer?

Pros

- Excellent for dealing with routine, repetitive clerical tasks
- Excellent for dealing with repetitive analytical tasks
- Excellent for dealing with repetitive reporting or information tasks
- Speeds up the provision of information
- Can integrate a number of aspects of business management
- Can improve service levels to customers
- The only way larger companies can now deal cost-effectively with managing their operations

Cons

- Large capital cost
- Large investment in time in putting your own operating systems on to computer and training staff to use it
- Unlikely to reduce staffing or administrative costs as you improve your service levels
- Can distract you from the main purpose of your business

The National Computing Centre (NCC)

The Centre is the UK Centre for Information Technology. Backed by, and in co-operation with, government, the IT industry and IT users, NCC directs technical programmes, administers national schemes and develops products and services to promote the effective use of IT.

The following five services are of particular interest to new computer users:

1. *Enquiry desk* for micro software - advice on the appropriate software packages for your system and organization.
2. *Micro software evaluation* - a new service for the independent evaluation and certification of micro software packages to a common standard.
3. *Software products scheme* - through which NCC has administered the allocation of £40 million to the development and marketing of 322 innovative software products.
4. *Selection testing service* - available on site and at fifteen locations throughout the UK, selection testing offers objective aptitute testing for all types of computer staff.
5. *Training* - NCC runs regular courses in most aspects of computers throughout the year at venues in London, Manchester, Glasgow, Bristol and Birmingham.

You can obtain further information from:

Head office
Tel: 061 228 6333
London and South East
Tel: 01 353 4875
Midlands
Tel: 021 236 6283
North and North Wales
Tel: 061 228 6333

Northern Ireland
Tel: 0232 665997
Scotland
Tel: 041 204 1101
South West and South Wales
Tel: 0272 277077

Federation of Microsystems Centres

The Federation was established in 1981 throughout Britain by the Department of Trade and Industry, National Computing Centre and local authorities, to provide impartial and expert advice to anyone thinking of first-time and subsequent computer purchase - and training. It is independent of computer suppliers and operates under a strict code of conduct, precluding computer sales and any commission payments.

The Centres offer a free initial discussion service to help clarify ideas and reduce the potential for inevitable pitfalls. Advice is offered at all stages: feasibility, requirements analysis, system selection, purchase negotiation and contracts, implementation, planning, training and acceptance.

Their training service is designed to help you and your staff to get the best out of your system, whether your company is large or small. They offer highly flexible programs, tailored to your needs, either using your own system or in the well-equipped training rooms at individual Centres.

In addition to structured training, a constantly updated library of self-study computer-related courses is available.

The Centres always keep a representative range of the most modern computers and applications for you to try out. Advice is also available on government grants which may benefit you. For general inquiries, you can telephone 091 276 6288 or contact your local centre.

Addresses of Microsystems Centres

Birmingham Microsystems Centre
Business Support Centre
Wolverley House
18 Digbeth
Birmingham
B5 6BJ
Tel: 021-631 4940

Business Resources Centre
Bolton Institute of Higher Education
Deane Road
Bolton
Lancashire
BL3 5AB
Tel: 0204-28851

Bristol Microsystems Centre
Bristol ITeC
St Anne's House
St Anne's Road
Bristol
BS4 4AB
Tel: 0272-779247

Cheltenham Microsystems Centre
GLOSCAT
Park Campus
Merestones Road
The Park
Cheltenham
Gloucester
GL50 2RR
Tel: 0242-532054/5

Dorset Microsystems Centre
Ground Floor
Holland House
Oxford Road
Bournemouth
BH8 8EZ
Tel: 0202-595400
0202-524111

Hampshire Microsystems Centre
Basingstoke Technical College
Worting Road
Basingstoke
RG1 1TN
Tel: 0256-471771

London Microsystems Centre
11 Clarke Path
Oldhill Place
London
N16 6QE
Tel: 01-802 1017

Newcastle Microsystems Centre
(Federation Administration Unit)
3 Heaton Road
Newcastle-upon-Tyne
NE6 1SA
Tel: 091-276 6288

Norwich Microsystems Centre
Ivory House Site
All Saints Green
Norwich
NR1 3NB
Tel: 0603-761076

South Yorkshire Microsystems Centre
Sheffield Science Park
Cooper Building
Arundel Street
Sheffield
S1 2NR
Tel: 0742-738184
0742-738258

Washington Microsystems Centre
Micro Technology Centre
Armstrong House
Armstrong Road
District 2
Washington
NE37 1PR
Tel: 091-417 8517

West Yorkshire Microsystems Centre
Leeds Polytechnic
Queenswood House
Beckett Park
Leeds
LS6 3QS
Tel: 0532-759741

Information Technology Centres (ITeCs)

ITeCs, as they are generally called, were first launched as an experiment in 1982, with the objective of encouraging unemployed youngsters to understand and make use of new technology. There are now 178 ITeCs covering the UK. They still have a major training role with young people and are an important source of employees to local businesses.

In addition they market their skills to surrounding companies offering drop-in training facilities in such fields as using business software packages.

ITeCs are supported in various ways by the Department of Trade and Industry, and Training Agency and local councils. The address of your nearest ITeC will be in the telephone directory.

The Association of Professional Computer Consultants

Founded in 1982, the Association has a Code of Professional Conduct which ensures that members' clients receive objective, impartial advice and services. Members are not allowed to supply (directly or indirectly) hardware or software, nor are they allowed to write software themselves for sale to their clients. They must not benefit from sales and agency commissions, introductory commissions, or trading links with computer industry suppliers. Contact the Association with details of your problem(s) and the sort of expertise you need and it will send you details of experienced independent and professional consultants, usually in your area.

The Association can be contacted at:

Association of Professional
Computer Consultants
109 Baker Street
London W1M 2BH
Tel: 01 907 8737

Computer Services Association (CSA)

The CSA is the trade association whose members offer bespoke and packaged software, data preparation, processing, consultancy, value-added network services, education and training, facilities management, third party maintenance, telecommunications and office automation. Its free Business Advisory Service will put you in touch with companies supplying the computing services you are looking for.

The Association can be contacted at:

CSA
Hanover House
73/74 High Holborn
London WC1V 6LE
Tel: 01 405 2171

Data Protection Registrar

The Registrar operates a telephone inquiry service for those concerned as to whether or not they should register. Alternatively, information packs on the Data Protection Act are available from post offices, and your trade association, chamber of commerce or local Microsystems Centre should be able to advise you.

You can contact the Registrar at:

Office of the Data Protection
Registrar
Springfield House
Water Lane
Wilmslow
Cheshire SK9 5AX
Tel: 0625 535711

2 Sources of Market Information

To succeed in business you need to build up an understanding of your customers and their needs and to develop a 'feel' for how the market might develop. Where will the opportunities and threats come in the future? What is happening to the market life-cycle? Is the market growing or declining? How are customers' tastes and preferences changing? Are your customers changing?

The most valuable source of information, which costs almost nothing, is your customers. You need to talk to them regularly, not just sell to them. You can find out from them what they think are your strenths and weaknesses, who they consider your major competitors, and the type of improvements they would like to see in your performance. Also, your suppliers and other people running local and small business can help.

However, a considerable amount of data is also available about companies, their products, services and markets. Much of this data is available through public sources but sometimes it must be paid for. There is a wealth of information from government statistics, newspapers, trade and technical journals, trade associations, statistics, reports, and so on. Business libraries can provide much of the information free of charge. Indeed, it has been said that the business libraries in London are the most extensive in their fields in Europe. The only investment you make is your time. However, if this is too much to expect there are many firms which offer to collect the data you need, for a fee. Remember that the cost of market information is likely to be much less than the cost of a relatively minor business mistake, a mistake that could prove fatal early in the life of a business.

If you intend to produce a business plan, perhaps to help you raise finance, it must be based on well-researched, accurate market information. It is one thing quietly to make mistakes, based upon ignorance; it is quite another to parade your lack of knowledge in front of bankers or financiers. If you are to produce a business plan, find out all you can about your customers, your competitors and your market-place before you start. Your research will pay handsome dividends.

Once you have an idea of the data that is available the next problem is to track it down. Fortunately many of the directories and publications are kept in the reference sections of major libraries.

The following organizations and publications contain key information on companies, products, markets and industries in the UK.

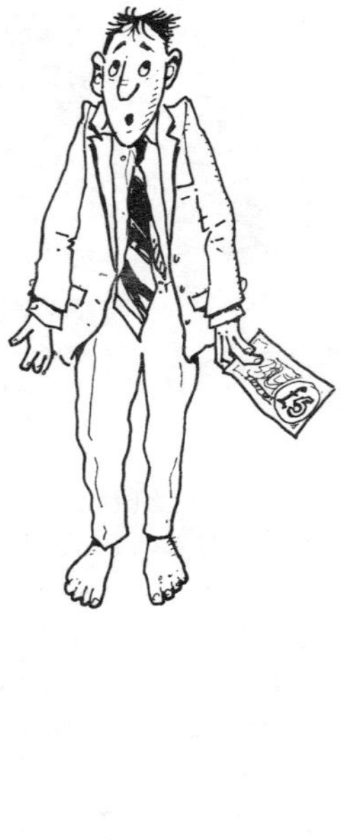

Why collect marketing information?

Pros	Cons
• It tells you about your customers • It tells you about your competitors • It tells you about your market-place • It is cheaper than making mistakes in business	• It can cost you both time and money to find the information • It is no substitute for direct contact with your customers

A. COMPANY INFORMATION

The following are the main sources from which you can obtain information.

The Centre for Interfirm Comparison

The Centre was established in 1959 by the British Institute of Management and the British Productivity Council to meet the need for a neutral expert body to conduct interfirm comparisons on a confidential basis, and to help managers to improve business performance. Participating firms feed a range of information into the Centre, which in turn feeds out yardsticks for them to compare systematically the performance of every important aspect of their business with other similar firms. Together with the yardstick ratios come written reports on the findings and ideas for action – but only, of course, to the participating firms, and even then only a 'comparative' basis so that no one company's data can ever be identified. The uniqueness of this method rests in part on the data itself. It goes far beyond anything supplied in companies' annual returns to Companies House or production monitor figures.

Thousands of companies, large and small have participated, and comparisons are made in over 100 industries, trades, services and professions both in the UK and abroad.

The Centre publishes a number of free booklets that explain its activities, the ratios it uses and why it uses those particular ratios and, more important, how you can use them to improve performance.

The Centre can be contacted at:

The Centre for Interfirm
Comparison
8 West Stockwell Street
Colchester
Essex C01 1HN
Tel: 0206 762274

Credit ratings

Giving credit to customers can provide to be very expensive, particularly when payment delays start to build up. The first step in an effective debtor control system is to choose reliable customers to offer credit to. To help firms do this a number of independent credit rating companies have been established which can provide financial and credit information on most companies of any size. This information is also valuable when it comes to assessing your competitors.

One such company is:

Credit Ratings Ltd
16–26 Banner Street
London EC1Y 8QE
Tel: 01 251 6675/6

The company provides an *ad hoc* subscription service called Credit Report. The cost varies from each report, depending on whether or not a commentary is wanted. These can normally be provided within forty-eight hours.

Each Credit Report provides a company profile, financial performance figures for the past two years, and eight credit ratios (including an estimate of how long the company normally takes to pay its bills). These ratios are then compared with the average for that industry, and are followed by a short commentary bringing important factors to the reader's attentions.

Other companies providing a similar service include:

Dun & Bradstreet International
Business Marketing Division
26-32 Clifton Street
London EC2P 2LY
Tel: 01 377 4377

Agricultural Credit Coporation Ltd
Agriculture House
Knightsbridge
London SW1X 7NJ
Tel: 01 235 6296

Infolink
Coombe Cross
2/4 South End
Croydon CR0 1DL
Tel: 01 686 7777

Provident Personal Credit Ltd
2 Kelly Street
London NW1 8PH
Tel: 01 485 7045

Companies Registration Office

The Registrar keeps records of all limited companies.

These records are kept at:

England and Wales
The Registrar of Companies
Crown Way
Maindy
Cardiff CF4 3UZ

Tel: 0222 388588

The Registrar of Companies
55 City Road
London EC1Y 11BB
Tel: 01 253 9393

Scotland
The Registrar of Companies for Scotland
102 George Street
Edinburgh EH2 3JD
Tel: 031 225 5774

For Northern Ireland the same service is available form:

The Department of Commerce
64 Chichester Street
Belfast BT1 4RJ
Tel: 0232 234488

The records kept include financial statements, accounts, directors' names and addresses, shareholders, and changes of name and structure. The information is available on microfiche or can be photocopied. This service is available to visitors only. There are a number of commercial organizations which will obtain this information for you.

Three such organizations are:

Jordan's Business Information Service
Jordan House
47 Brunswick Place
London N1 6EE
Tel: 01 253 3030

Express Company Registrations
Express House
6 Baches Street
London N1 6VB
Tel: 01 253 5323

Oyez Professional Services
Classic House
174/180 Old Street
London EC1V 9BP
Tel: 01 251 4708

Datastream service

Financial information on companies is provided through on-line terminals by Datastream. This facility is usually available through your nearest business library.

Extel quoted service

Cards are published each year by the Exchange Telegraph Co Ltd. Cards for each of the 3,000 UK companies quoted on the Stock Exchange contain comprehensive information on the company including financial results, directors, bankers, auditors, solicitors, share price, and chairman's report. The unquoted service covers some 2,000 ordinary companies and those on the USM, OTL and Third Market.

Individual cards can be bought from:

Extel Statistical Service Ltd
37/45 Paul Street
London EC2A 4PB
Tel: 01 253 3400

McCarthy information services

McCarthy provides a comprehensive press comment service monitoring the daily and financial press. From some fifty papers and journals it extracts information on quoted companies each day and unquoted companies each week. The service is provided on annual subscription. Alternatively, an on-line and microfiche service are also offered.

McCarthy can be contacted at:

McCarthy Information Ltd
Manor House
Ash Walk
Warminster
Wilts BA12 8PY
Tel: 0985 215151

The Retail Directory

This directory gives details of over 1,300 department stores and nearly 5,000 private shops. It gives the names of executives and merchandise buyers, as well as addresses and telephone numbers, early closing days, etc. It also covers multiple shops, co-operative societies, supermarkets and many other retail outlets. There is a useful survey, showing retail activities on each major shopping street in the country. It gives the name and nature of the retail business in each street.

A separate volume contains shop surveys for the Greater London area, with nearly 30,000 shops listed by name, street number and trade. The head offices of over 1,000 multiples are given, as are up to 250 surveys showing what sort of shops are in any area. This can be used for giving sales people useful contacts within their territory.

The Directory is published by:

Newman Publishing Ltd
48 Poland Street
London W1V 4PP
Tel: 01 439 0335

Who Owns Whom (UK)

Volume I lists parent companies, showing the structure of a group as a whole and the relationship with member companies. Volume II lists subsidiaries and associates showing their parent companies.

The publisher is:

Dun & Bradstreet
26-32 Clifton Steet
London EC2P 2LY
Tel: 01 377 4377

B. PRODUCT INFORMATION

Kelly's Business Directory

Kelly's has an alphabetical list of manufacturers, merchants, wholesalers and firms, together with their trade descriptions, addresses, and telephone and telex number. Entries are also listed by trade classification. The directory covers 90,000 UK firms classified under 10,000 trade, product or service headings. There is also a section giving an alphabetical listing of brand and trade names, showing the name of the manufacturer or UK distributor and a brief description of the product.

Kelly's is published by:

Kelly's Directories
Windsor Court
East Grinstead House
East Grinstead
West Sussex RH19 1XF
Tel: 0342 326972

Key British Enterprises

KBE contains information on 20,000 UK companies that between them are responsible for 90 per cent of industrial expenditure. As well as the name, address and telephone and telex numbers of the main office of each company, it gives branch addresses, products indexed by SIC code, sales turnovers (UK and overseas), directors' names and responsibilities, shareholders, capital structure, trade names and number of employees.

> *KBE is in three volumes with updates; it is published by:*
>
> Dun & Bradstreet Ltd
> 26–32 Clifton Street
> London EC2P 2LY
> Tel: 01 377 4377

Kompass

Published in association with the CBI in four volumes: Volumes I and II are indexed by product or service to help find suppliers, indicating whether they are manufacturers, wholesalers or distributors.

Volume III gives basic company information on the 30,000 suppliers identified from Volume I. These include the addresses, telephone and telex numbers, bankers, directors, office hours and the number of employees.

Volume IV gives financial data on these companies over a three-year period giving: turnover, profit before tax, fixed assets, current assets, shareholders' funds and the ultimate holding company, if any.

It is expensive, but available at most business libraries.

> *For further details contact:*
>
> Kompass Publishers
> Windsor Court
> East Grinstead House
> East Grinstead
> West Sussex RH19 1XD
> Tel: 0342 326972

Mintel

A monthly publication providing reports on the performance of new products and a wide range of specific areas of consumer expenditure, *Mintel* covers several specific consumer goods markets each month, combining published data and original research to make the studies as exhaustive as possible.

Comprehensive data on leisure and retail markets is also given. Mintel provides research services and has an on-line service.

Further details from:

Mintel Publications Ltd
18 Long Lane
London EC1A 9HE
Tel: 01 606 4533

Organizations offering advice on design

The following organizations can offer further advice and publications, if approached directly:

Department of Trade and Industry
Ebury Bridge House
2–18 Ebury Bridge Road
London SW1W 8QD
Tel: 01 215 5000

(also local DTI Regional Offices)

The Design Council
28 Haymarket
London SW1Y 4SU
Tel: 01 839 8000

Chartered Society of Designers
29 Bedford Square
London WC1B 3EG
Tel:01 631 1510

Insitution of Engineering Designers
Courtleigh
Westbury Leigh
Westbury
Wilshire BA13 3TA
Tel: 0373 822801

Engineering Industry Training Board
54 Clarendon Road
Watford
Hert WD1 1LB
Tel: 0923 38441

C. MARKET AND INDUSTRY INFORMATION

Annual Abstract of Statistics

This publication is the basic source of all UK statistics. Figures are given for each of the preceding ten years, so trends can be recognized.

It is published by:

The Central Statistical Office
Great George Street
London SW1 3AL
Tel 01 270 6363

Business Briefings

Published weekly, Business Briefings provides a regular monitor of business statistics, news, regulations, and information of sources. These include the private sector, Europe, and government departments such as DTI, Employment, Environment, Transport, Energy, Treasury, Internal Revenue, Customs and Excise, together with vital information for both importers and exporters.

For further information contact:

Association of British Chambers of Commerce,
Sovereign House
212 Shaftesbury Avenue
LONDON
WC2H 8EW
Tel: 01 240 5831/6

Business Monitors

The medium through which the government publishes the business statistics it collects from over 20,000 UK firms, the *Business Monitors* are the primary, and very often the only, source of detailed information on the sectors they cover. The *Monitors* can help businessmen to monitor trends and trace the progress of 4,000 individual products, manufactured by firms in 160 industries. *Monitors* can also be used to rate your business performance against that of your industry and measure the efficiency of different parts of your business.

The *Monitors* are published in three main series. The *Production Monitors* are published monthly, quarterly and annually. The quarterly is probably the most useful, with comprehensive yet timely information. The *Service and Distribution Monitors* cover the retail market, the instalment credit business, the montor trade, catering and allied trades and the computer service industry, among others. Finally, there are *Miscellaneous Monitors* covering such topics as shipping, insurance, import/export ratios for industry, acquistions and mergers of industrial and commercial companies, cinemas and tourism.

The *Annual Census of Production Monitor* covers virtually every sector of industry, and includes data on total purchase, total sales, stocks, work in progress, capital expenditure, employment, wages and salaries. It includes analyses of costs and output, of establishments by size, of full- and part-time employees by sex, and of employment, net capital expenditure and net output by region.

The Monitors can be purchased from:

HMSO
PO Box 276
London SW8 5DT
Enquires Tel: 01 873 0011
Orders Tel: 01 873 9090

Family Expenditure Survey

Published by HMSO, the FES shows in great detail income and expenditure by type of household for the UK and includes some regional analyses.

Guide to Official Statistics

The main guide to all government produced statistics, including *ad hoc* reports, it is published by HMSO.

A brief free guide is available each year from:

The Press, Publicity and Publications Division
Central Statistical Office
Great George Street
London SW1 3AL
Tel: 01 270 6363

ICC Business Ratios

ICC produces 200 business sector reports analysing the performance of some 12,000 leading UK companies over a three-year period. For each business sector nineteen key performance ratios are shown for each company in the sector and an average for the sector as a whole.

Further details are available from:

The Business Ratio Manager
ICC Business Ratios
28–42 Banner Street
London EC1Y 8QE
Tel: 01 253 3906

Jordan's Business Information Service

Jordan's also produces a range of annual business surveys covering some fifty industries. It's Company Search Department can obtain information for you on any UK company in Companies House, and the Rapid Reply Service can guarantee dispatch within a few hours. Alternatively, if you really are in a hurry, Jordan's has a telex and telephone service.

Information from:

Jordan's Business Information Service
Jordan House
21 St Thomas Street
Bristol BS1 6JS
Tel: 0272 230600

Key Note Publications

Key Note produces concise briefs on 100 market sectors of the UK economy.

Each *Key Note* contains a detailed examination of the structure of an industry, its distribution network and its major companies; an in-depth analysis of the market, covering products by volume and value, market shares, foreign trade and an appraisal of trends within the market; a review of recent developments in the industry, highlighting new product

development, corporate development and legislation; a financial analysis of named major companies, providing data and ratios over a three-year period, together with a corporate appraisal and economic overview; forecasts on the future prospects for the industry, including estimates from Key Note's own database and authoritative trade sources. There is a very useful appendix detailing further sources of information - recent press articles, other reports and journals.

Key Note can be contacted at:

Key Note Publications
Field House
72 Oldfield Road
Hampton
Middx TW12 2HG
Tel: 01 783 0755

McCarthy's industry service

The industry service is a comprehensive press cutting service, classified into fourteen industry groups: agricultural and animal and vegetable raw materials; building and civil engineering; finance; general engineering; electrical and electronic engineering; chemicals and chemical engineering; miscellaneous industrial manufacturers; consumer goods manufacture; transport and transport equipment; marketing; distribution and consumer services; communications and communications equipment; mining and minerals; and energy. Within the main industry group lie about 350 subsections. Marketing, for example, ranges from auto-vending, franchising to street markets, as well as the more predictable department stores and supermarket groups.

Press cuttings are provided.
These can be obtained from:

McCarthy Information Ltd
Manor House
Ash Walk
Warminster
Wilts BA12 8PY
Tel: 0985 215151

Office of Population Censuses and Surveys (OPCS)

The OPCS produces demographic statistics for each country in England and Wales from the 1981 census (next census in 1991). These provide data not only on total populations in each area, but also on occupations, economic groups, etc. Similar reports from Scottish and Northern Ireland regions are also available.

There is a reference library at:

OPCS
St Catherine House
10 Kingsway
London WC2B 6JP
Telephone: 01 242 0262

More information and answers to general inquiries on these reports are also available from the same number.

Social Trends

Published by HMSO, *Social Trends* brings together key social and demographic data on many aspects of the UK economy. It contains useful charts and graphs.

D. PLACES TO FIND THE INFORMATION

Much of the information listed earlier can be found in many of the major reference libraries throughout the country. The following is a list of the libraries with a particularly comprehensive selection of business information.

British Institute of Management Library and Management Information Centre

The library houses one of the largest specialist collections of management literature in Europe. This includes much valuable information not generally available. The services are for BIM members, who may use the library in person or make inquiries by letter or telephone.

The library also produces extremely valuable reading lists covering a wide range of topics. These provide a selective guide to books, directories and periodicals in any of 170 specific areas. It also publishes *A Basic Library of Management*, which lists 300 or so of the more useful books in the management field.

The library is at:

Management House
Cottingham Road
Corby
Northants NN17 1TT
Tel: 0536 204222
Open Monday to Friday,
0900–1700

Central Statistical Office Library

This library keeps all the data produced in published form by the Business Statistics Office, together with a substantial quantity of non-official material. The coverage extends beyond UK statistics to include foreign information on an extensive range of company data and trade directories.

The library is freely open to the public, who can inquire personally or by telephone, telex or letter.

The library is situated at:

Central Statistical Office Library
Cardiff Road
Newport
Gwent NP9 1XG
Tel: 0633 812973
Open Monday to Friday,
0900–1700

Chartered Institute of Marketing

The Institute has the largest and most comprehensive marketing information library in the UK. This and its other services are provided for its members.

The library is situated at:

Chartered Institute of Marketing
Moor Hall
Cookham
Maidenhead
Berks SL6 9QH
Tel: 06285-24922

The British Library

Science Reference and Information Service

This is the national library for modern science and technology, for patents, trade marks and designs. It has the most comprehensive reference section of this type of literature in Western Europe. If you do not have an adequate library close at hand a visit here could save you visits to several libraries. It should also be able to provide you with answers if most other places cannot do so.

The Library's resources are formidable. It has 25,000 different journals, with issues back to 1960, on open shelves and the rest quickly available. It has 85,000 books and pamphlets and 20,250,000 patents. It has a worldwide collection of journals on trade marks, together with books on law and design. Most of the major UK and European reports are held, as is trade literature and around 1,000 abstracting periodicals.

The services are equally extensive. You may visit without prior arrangement or a reader's ticket. Telephone requests for information, including the checking of references, are accepted. Once at the library, staff are available to help you find items and to answer general queries. Scientific staff are also on hand for specialized inquiries. There is even a linguist service to help you inspect material written in a foreign language, though for this service you must make an appointment.

The service is situated at:

The British Library
Science Reference and
Information Service
25 Southampton Buildings
Chancery Lane
London WC2A 1AY
Tel: 01 323 7497/7496
Open Monday–Friday,
0930–2100; Saturday, 1000–1300
Patent inquiries: 01 323 7919
Subscription inquiry service: 01
323 7979 (0900–1700)
Free service for brief inquiries: 01
323 7454

The Business Information Service

Set up in 1981 in response to demand for a national business information service, this service specializes in the provision of market, company and product information. Personal callers to the library receive help with their inquiries from specialist staff. A charged business information service and on-line searching service for more detailed research are also offered.

The service is at:

The British Library
Business Information Service
Science Reference and
Information Service
25 Southampton Buildings
Chancery Lane
London WC2A 1AW
Tel: 01 323 7979
Open Monday–Friday, 0930–1700
Free service for brief inquiries: 01
323 7464

Official Publications Library

Virtually all official British publications are held here, together with an extensive intake from all other countries of the world and from international organizations. All the UK and major overseas series complementing the Statistics and Market Intelligence Library are here too. An extensive world-wide collection of legislative publications and a complete set of all current UK electoral registers are kept here.

The Library is situated at:

The British Library
Business Information Service
Science Reference and
Information Service
25 Southampton Buildings
Chancery Lane
London WC2A 1AW
Tel: 01 323 7979
Open Monday–Friday, 0930–1700
Free service for brief inquiries: 01 323 7464

The Newspaper Library

A comprehensive set of British (national and local) newspapers and most major foreign and commonwealth newspapers are kept here. It is best to telephone and check the Library has what you want, or you can send for a catalogue and price list.

The Library is at:

The British Library
Official Publications Library
Great Russell Street
London WC1B 3DG
Tel: 01 636 1544
Open Monday, Friday, Saturday
0930–1645; Tuesday–Thurday
0930–2045
(Visitors should telephone first)

Export Market Information Centre

The centre is primarily concerned with statistics and directories from overseas countries and import/export data on the UK. As such, it is the most important source of international statistics and business information.

It is situated at:

1 Victoria Street,
London SW1H 0ET
Tel 01 215 5444/5
Reading room open
Monday–Friday, 0930–1730

In addition to these special libraries, major chambers of commerce, such as those in London, Leeds, Birmingham, Edinburgh, Manchester, Bristol and Glasgow, have their own substantial business collections.

E. INFORMATION SERVICES

The following organizations can help businesses to find marketing information.

The Financial Times Business Information Service

The service offers impartial, authoritative facts – facts about companies, industries, statistics and people. Press cuttings on some 25,000 prominent people in industry, politics and business are kept, and there is a Business Information Consultancy, which can offer an on-demand information service to meet individual information requirements.

The service is available to subscribers only. Subscriptions are on a six-month or annual basis; prices vary with the level of service required.

Information may be obtained from:

FT Business Information Service
1 Southwark Bridge
London SE1 9HL
Tel 01 873 3000

Industrial Aids

This service is geared to supply commercial and technical information, such as: Who makes what/where/how much? Who is company A's agent in country X? Where are custom manufacturing sources? Details are given of company financial data, affiliations, product literature, consumption patterns, end users, prices, discounts and trading terms, as well as new legislation and standards, trade and industrial economic statistics, conference papers, proceedings and lists of delegates.

Inquiry service at:

14 Buckingham Palace Road
London SW1W 0QP
Tel: 01 828 5036

Market Location

Market Location is a research organization studying manufacturing industry in the UK. It gathers its information through field research. Its team of researcher travel the country, marking each manufacturing unit on maps and conducting a face-to-face interview with a representative of the company in order to obtain accurate, first-hand information.

The data gathered is published on a series of large-scale maps with accompanying indexes, giving the company name, address and telephone number; the name of the location manager and his or her position; the activity of the company and its SIC main-order heading; the size of the workforce and the company's group structure.

Clients of Market Location are usually companies with a sales force selling to manufacturing industry. They use the service to improve their sales performance by finding new prospects, by increasing salespeople's call rates, reducing travelling expenses, and eliminating potentially abortive cold-calling.

Market Location produces statistics tables for each country, showing the number of factories, broken down by SIC code and number of employees (including percentages).

Information may be obtained from:

Market Location Ltd
1 Warwick Street
Leamington Spa
Warwicks CV32 5LW
Tel: 0926 334235

The Market Research Society

This is the professional body for those concerned with market, social and economic research. It has 3,500 members and is the largest body of its kind in the world.

Apart from a programme of education, research and publications of primary interest to members, the Society produces a directory of organizations providing market research services. The directory provides background information on the 210 research agencies, their executives, experience and size in sales turnover. Some of the organizations are quite small, with turnovers below £50,000 per annum, whereas others have a turnover of several million pounds. The Society also publishes the *International Research Directory*:

The Society's address is:

The Market Research Society
175 Oxford Street
London W1R 1TA
Tel: 01 439 2585

The Marketing Shop

This organization provides a wide range of marketing services, but its Information Service is perhaps the most useful facility for small businesses. It can provide data on practically any topic, either using its own library or outside sources, and will also monitor the media for information on companies, products or markets. Charges are at an hourly rate for *ad hoc* work. The more usual arrangement is for customers to take a block of hours to be used over the year. Block fees work out at a much lower hourly rate. In general the shop will give a quotation for any research it does.

It may be contacted at:

The Marketing Shop
18 Kingly Court
Kingly Street
London W1R 5LE
Tel: 01 434 2671

Warwick Business Information Services

The service offers a range of commerical and economic information based on published sources including international statistics, both official and non-official, market research, periodicals, reports, directories, company reports and on-line service.

The service will also undertake analysis of the data in question, and provides a written report on its desk reseach.

Annual subscribers to the service pay a fixed rate for ten hours' search time and the results. Occasional users of the service can obtain information or research assistance on an *ad hoc* basis at a rather higher hourly rate, subject to a minimum charge. All in all, it is very good value.

The address is:

Warwick Business Information Services
University of Warwick Library
Coventry CV4 7AL
Tel: 0203 523251

F. ON-LINE DATABASES

There are now nearly 3,000 databases via 500 services, worldwide. These are listed and described in the definitive on-line directory.

The directory is available from:

Cuadra Associates
2001 Wilshire Boulevard
Suite 305
Santa Monica
California WA
USA

Closer to home, ASLIB can help on most aspects of on-line searching.

It may be contacted at:

ASLIB
20–24 Old Street
London EC1V 9AP
Tel: 01 253 4488

Useful business databases include the following:

Datasolve

Datasolve sells the *World Reporter*, which contains reports from the *Financial Times*, *The Economist*, BBC World Service, etc. It also offers 'World Exporter', a foreign market intelligence service.

Its address is:

Datasolve
99 Staines Road West
Sunbury-on-Thames
Middx TW16 7AH
Tel: 0932 785566

Dialog

A major publisher of technical, business and financial information, worldwide, its EUSIDIC Database Guide lists more databases.

It may be contacted at:

Dialog
Learned Information
PO Box 188
Oxford OX1 5AX
Tel: 0865 730275

Echo

Echo provides technical and commercial information on the EC.

It may be contacted at:

Echo
177 Route d'Esch
1471 Luxembourg
Tel: 010 352 488041

Fintext

A financial information service on British Telecom's Prestel service, which offers guidance on sources and uses of finance, tax planning and management advice, pension scheme, guides to computer hardware and software, and the London Enterprise Agency's LINK marriage bureau – a business introduction service bringing investors and fund-seekers together.

ICC Online

ICC provides financial information on companies, together with industry averages, for comparison purposes.

Its address is:

ICC Database
ICC Information Group Ltd
Field House
72 Oldfield Road
Hampton
Middx TW12 2HQ
Tel: 783 1122

Mead Data

Mead publishes, among others, an international legal information service, LEXIS.

It may be contacted at:

Mead Data
1 St Katherine's Way
London E1 9UN
Tel: 01 488 9187

Pergamon Financial Data Services

Key British Enterprises, *Who Owns Whom* and various management and marketing abstracts.

It may be contacted at:

Pergamon Financial Data
Services
Achilles House
Western Avenue
London W3 0UA
Tel: 01 992 3456

G. FRANCHISING

A franchise is a business relationship in which the owner of the name or method of doing business allows a local operator to set up a business under that name. The local operator (the franchisee) pays the parent organization (the franchisor) an initial fee and, usually, a continuing royalty for the privilege.

The franchisor lays down a blueprint on how the business should be operated – the content and nature of the goods/services being offered; price and performance standards; type, size and layout of premises; design of stationery; staffing and operating procedures. The franchisor also provides the franchisee with training and other back-up support.

Franchising is one of the most popular ways to expand an existing business, once the formula has been proven. The market is worth some £3 billion, taken up by 400 franchisors with around 20,000 outlets between them. Over half these franchisors entered the market within the last five years. Some, like the Body Shop, Sock Shop and Tie Rack, have been spectacularly successful, reaching the stock market in a fraction of the time taken by companies pursuing a more conventional strategy.

Should you set up franchises?

Pros

- You obtain a rapid increase in your market penetration with little capital commitment
- You deal with highly motivated customers – the franchisees – who are keen to maximize sales
- You do not have to stretch your own organizational skills. Once trained, you should be able to delegate to the franchisee. You also save on administration
- You probably will not face union or other associated labour problems in your expansion
- You do not share the franchisee's business risks
- You obtain an initial franchise fee and a regular income from your franchisees

Cons

- You do not have as close control over a franchisee as an employee and, consequently, an individual franchisee may reflect badly on the franchise operation as a whole
- Franchisees can actually become too independent and regularly set up in business on their own. To succeed, any franchise must continue to provide mutual benefit for franchisee and franchisor

Organizations

The following organizations can help you with your plans to set up a franchise chain.

The British Franchise Association

The Association was formed in 1977 to establish a clear definition of ethical franchising standards, and to help members of the public, press, potential investors and government bodies to differentiate between sound business opportunities and suspect business offers. It currently has some seventy members. Although being a member of the BFA does not guarantee the likely success of a franchise, it does show acceptance of a code of practice.

The Association will provide a checklist of questions to ask a franchisor, and will answer questions on non-BFA companies if it has the information.

It may be contacted at:

Thames View
Newton Road
Henley-on-Thames
Oxfordshire RG9 1HG
Tel: 0491 578049

The European Franchise Federation

The Federation may be contacted at:

The European Franchise Federation
Avenue de Broqueville 5
B/1150 Brussels
Tel: (32) 27366464

Franchise consultants

These companies can advise you on the suitability of your business to the franchising approach. A list of consultants can be obtained from the British Franchise Association.

Three important questions you should ask anyone offering their services in this field are:

1. Has the consultant been involved in successful franchising at a high level?
2. Has the consultant demonstrated his or her ability to advise? Ask to speak to some of his or her past clients.
3. Is the consultant taking commission on the sale of the franchises his or her client is launching? If so, there could well be an undesirable conflict of interest.

Lawyers listed by members

Lawyers can help you with the legal aspects of drawing up franchise contracts for your franchisees. A list of franchise lawyers can be obtained from the British Franchise Association.

Banks and other financial institutions

These companies can provide general advice to franchisors, fund the development of a franchise concept and provide some of the money your franchises will need to buy their franchise from you. Most franchise chains have a link with a financial institution to provide franchisees with up to two-thirds of the cost of a franchise.

A list of banks specializing in this field can be obtained from the British Franchise Association.

Accountants

Accountancy firms can help you to prepare financial projections showing the viability of your concept and help at all stages of the development of a franchise.

A list of accounts specializing in franchising can be obtained from the British Franchise Association.

3 Financial Assistance and Other Assistance

There is a plethora of schemes offering financial and other business assistance to smaller firms. You might be eligible for cash grants or subsidized loan schemes for certain types of investment in certain areas. Other schemes aim to offer subsidized advice or consultancy for certain types of activities. Many areas of the country offer special schemes to help smaller businesses secure premises at preferential rents. Indeed, so many schemes are now on offer that it is quite a problem finding your way through the maze.

There are relatively few national grants for smaller businesses. Most grants are intended to attract firms to certain parts of the country. The government offers grants in its 'Designated Development Areas' and 'Intermediate Areas'. These can overlap with schemes offered by local authorities and, indeed, special schemes in Scotland, Wales and Northern Ireland. The various bodies set up to encourage this local development have also developed a range of other incentives to attract business to their part of the country. Each scheme seems to have been designed to meet local needs. The problem is to know what is on offer in any particular part of the country.

This chapter is organized into seven sections:

A. National assistance.
B. Regional assistance.
C. England.
D. Scotland.
E. Wales.
F. Northern Ireland.
G. Local authorities and other local initiatives.

To decide which schemes might apply to you, you should first check Section A, since these schemes are open to all eligible firms. Then, check

Section B to see if you fall within one of the regions in which special schemes apply. Next, refer to Section C, D, E *or* F, depending upon your location. Finally, check with Section G to see whether your local area has any special schemes. You should not need to look through more than four of these sections.

By checking through the schemes that apply to you, in your particular industry in your particular part of the country, you should be able to cut through the maze, and save yourself a great deal of time and effort.

A. NATIONAL ASSISTANCE

Apart from the relatively generous assistance to businesses located or locating in particular regions of the UK, a number of grants and other forms of assistance and advice are available nationwide. This section summarizes the principal schemes on offer, listed under the main sector of the economy served, activity covered, or the organization providing the assistance. These are by no means the only grant aid schemes on offer, but are the ones considered of most importance to our intended audience.

The Enterprise Initiative

This is the title of the Department of Trade and Industry's (DTI) flagship programme, launched in January 1988, with the objective of making available best business practice to independent firms with fewer than 500 employees. In general the financial assistance offered under this initiative is confined to some free, and some heavily subsidized, professional consultancy.

Business Review

This is the entry point to the initiative, and through the Business Review eligible firms can have up to two days' free consultancy carried out by a specially appointed enterprise counsellor, whose role is to help the client's business to assess its strengths and weaknesses, to identify the constraints on growth and to assess the need for specialist advice through the most relevant initiative.

Consultancy Initiative

There are six initiatives: Marketing, Design, Quality, Manufacturing, Business Planning, and Financial and Information Systems. Firms are signposted to the most appropriate initiative via the Business Review, whose consultants will in turn work with clients to draw up terms of reference.

Eligible firms can take up to two initiatives. The DTI is budgeted to support 1,000 consultations a week under the six schemes.

The DTI will pay half the cost of between five and fifteen man-days of consultancy. In assisted areas and Urban Programme areas, it will pay two-thirds. (The boundaries of these areas change from time to time, but your local DTI office can advise on the current situation.)

Marketing Initiative

This initiative is managed by the Insitute of Marketing and conducted on its behalf by a number of regional centres. Specialists can help to identify the most profitable markets either at home or abroad; help to find out how customers needs and demands are changing; look at policies in connection with pricing, distribution and after-sales service - and competition. The Marketing Initiative is intended to leave clients with a comprehensive marketing plan.

Design Initiative

Managed by the Design Council, this initiative offers expert advice on design from product concept to corporate image. It can help with:

(a) product innovation and feasibility studies;
(b) design for efficient production;
(c) mechanical and electrical engineering design;
(d) selection and use of materials;
(e) industrial design and styling;
(f) product safety and ergonomic considerations;
(g) packaging and point of sale material;
(h) corporate identity.

Quality Initiative

Managed by the Production Engineering Research Association (PERA) and in the North-West by Salford University Business Services Ltd, this initiative offers expert advice on introducing an appropriate quality management system and so keep both standards and output at satisfactory and profitable levels.

Manufacturing Initiative

Also managed by PERA, this initiative seeks, by the effective introduction of modern manufacturing methods and systems, to reduce stock and release valuable cash.

Business Planning Initiative

Managed by Investors in Industry, this initiative was launched in April 1988 to provide expert advice on the development of business plans. This process involves a review of business objectives and competitive strategies.

Financial and Information Systems Initiative

Also managed by Investors in Industry, this initiative provides expert advice on improving existing budgeting and financial control systems, or designing and introducing new ones. It will also include a review of accounting records, the use of data services and any computer and software needs.

For further information on any of these six initiatives contact one of the regional offices of the DTI, listed in Section B: Regional assistance.

The Enterprise Allowance Scheme

This scheme, provided by the Department of Employment, is intended to help unemployed people who want to start up in business but who may be deterred from doing so by the fact that they lose their entitlement to unemployment or supplementary benefit.

Applicants must be eighteen or over, under retirement age, have been unemployed for at least eight weeks, and be receiving unemployment or supplementary benefit at the time of applying. They must also be prepared to work full time, and will be required to demonstrate that they have at least £1,000 available which they intend to invest in the business. The business must be new. The allowance – a flat rate of £40 a week – is paid fortnightly for a maximum of fifty-two weeks, and is regarded as taxable. The scheme is being operated by Jobcentre with the help of the Department of Employment's Small Firms Service, whose counsellors provide advice and free guidance to those entering the scheme.

Further information on all Department of Employment Schemes may be obtained from the local Jobcentre or Employment Office, or from the appropriate Department of Employment regional office, the addresses of which are listed below.

Department of Employment regional offices

East Midlands Regional Office
The Training Agency
21–23 Castlegate
Nottingham NG7 7AG
Tel: 021 456 1144

South West Regional Office
The Training Agency
The Pithay
Bristol BS1 2NQ
Tel: 0272 294030

London Regional Office
The Training Agency
236 Grays Inn Road
London WC1 8HL
Tel: 01 278 0363

Northern Regional Office
The Training Agency
Wellbar House
Gallowgate
Newcastle upon Tyne NE1 4TD
Tel: 091 232 7575

North West Regional Office
The Training Agency
Washington House
Capital Centre
New Bailey Street
Manchester M3 5ER
Tel: 061 833 0251

South East Regional Office
The Training Agency
Telford House
Hamilton Close
Basingstoke
Tel: 0256 29266

West Midlands Regional Office
The Training Agency
Alpha Tower
Suffolk Street
Queensway
Birmingham
B1 1UR

Yorkshire and Humberside Regional Office
The Training Agency
City House
New Station Street
Leeds LS1 4JA
Tel: 0532 438232

Office for Scotland
The Training Agency
9 St Andrew Square
Edinburgh EH2 2QX
Tel: 031 225 8500

Office for Wales
The Training Agency
Companies House
Crown Way
Maindy
Cardiff CF4 3UT
Tel: 0222 388588

Research and development

Research and Technology Initiative

Through this initiative the DTI will provide up to 50 per cent of the funds needed to enable a project involving collaborative research between firms or between firms and researchers in scientific and educational institutes, to go ahead.

The projects must be innovative, technically realistic and have a good chance of eventual commercial exploitation.

Small Firms Merit Award for Research and Technology (SMART)

This is a competition-based award, providing up to 100 grants each year for firms with less than 200 employees. (New start-ups are also eligible.) The maximum grant will be for 75 per cent (up to £37,500) towards the cost of developing a product or process involving new technology. The technology should be innovative, but have a good chance of developing into a viable business. Winners can go on to a second stage in the following years. Regional offices of the DTI, listed above, can provide details of these schemes.

EC initiatives

The European Community provides grants to industry (and others) for research and development. Several programmes have gained public recognition recently. These include:

1. ESPRIT – the European Strategic Programme for Research and Development in Information Technology.
2. BRITE – Basic Research in Industrial Technologies for Europe.
3. RACE – Research in Advanced Communications Technologies for Europe.

Businesses interested should monitor the *Official Journal* of the Commission and watch for public invitations to submit project proposals. If successful the Commission usually funds up to 50 per cent of the eligible costs.

For further information contact:

DGXII
Commissioin for The European Communities
Rue de la Loi 200
1049 Brussels
Belgium

The Environment Programme

The EC provides grants of between 30 and 75 per cent of the cost of projects that:

(a) are aimed at developing new clean technologies, waste recycling, reuse technologies, or locating and restoring contaminated sites,
(b) seek to develop new technologies and methods of measuring and monitoring the natural environment;
(c) contribute towards the maintenance or re-establishment of seriously threatened areas.

Environmental Protection Technology Scheme (EPT)

A new government-backed grant provides between 25 and 50 per cent of the costs of projects that are likely to lead to an improved stardard of environmental protection, and that would not otherwise have gone ahead.

For further information on either of the two schemes above, contact:

Department of the Environment
Romney House
43 Marsham Street
London SW1P 3EB
Tel: 01 276 3000

Energy conservation

Energy Efficiency Surveys (EES)

A government grant of up to 50 per cent of the consultancy costs is available towards the cost of extended surveys of business premises by energy experts and for combined heat and power (CHP) feasibility studies. There is a limit of twenty extended surveys per applicant and £10,000 per study.

For further information contact:

Energy Efficiency Office
Department of Energy
1 Palace Street
London SW1E 5HE
Tel: 01 273 3000

Energy Efficiency Demonstration Scheme

A grant of 25 per cent of the instaled capital cost of implementing innovative technology which will lead to the more efficient use of energy is available to business enterprises (non-nationalized), who in turn must allow the scheme to be monitored by the Energy Efficiency Office. They must also be prepared to allow visitors to see the project at work and to allow publication and promotion of results. Any reasonable costs incurred in accommodating such observations will be met by the grant body.

The projects themselves must:

(a) be aimed at promoting the more effective use of energy and should lead to substantial benefits on a national scale;
(b) achieve a benefit that is significant in relation to the grant given;
(c) achieve savings that will be attractive to others in the industry, using current investment criteria;
(d) be unable to proceed without the grant.

For information on buildings contact:	*For all other information contact:*
Inquiries Bureau Building Research Energy Conservation Support Unit Building Research Establishment Bucknells Lane Garston Watford Herts WD2 7JR Tel: 0923 894040	Inquiries Bureau Energy Support Unit Building 156 Harwell Laboratory Didcot Oxon OX11 0RA Tel: 0235 821000

Tourism

Grants of up to 25 per cent of capital costs are available for tourism projects that will attract tourists from the UK and abroad; increase tourist spending or make their stay more agreeable; directly or indirectly create new jobs; be more likely to create new markets rather than just displacing existing business.

Individual grants cannot exceed £200,000 without approval from the appropriate government department, nor can public sector funds from all sources exceed 50 per cent of costs.

In addition to grants, repayable grants and loans for up to ten years are also available. All assistance is conditional on there being no alternative source of funds.

Tourist boards in their capacity as agents for the European Investment Bank can make loans in the Assisted Areas (see Section B: Regional assistance) of up to £2.5 million for tourist projects.

For further information contact:

English Tourist Board 26 Grosvenor Gardens London SW1W 0DV Tel: 01 730 3450	Scottish Tourist Board 23 Ravelston Terrace Edinburgh EH4 3EU Tel: 031 332 2433
Wales Tourist Board Brunel House 2 Fitzalan Road Cardiff CF2 1UY Tel: 0222 499909	Northern Ireland Tourist Board River House 48 High Street Belfast Tel: 0232 231221

The Highlands and Islands Development Board can provide grants and other assistance in its own region (see Section D: Scotland for details).

Crafts Council

Formed as the Crafts Advisory Committee in 1971, in 1979 it became known as the Crafts Council. It is a registered charity and incorporated under Royal Charter. Members serve at the invitation of the Minister for Arts. It receives an annual grant from the Office of Arts and Libraries with which to support the crafts in England and Wales. The Council offers business advice and finance to artists and craftsmen and women as well as a subsidy for craft projects. It has a 'setting up scheme' to help with the costs of setting up a first workshop. In Scotland the responsibility for crafts rests with the Scottish Development Agency.

For further information contact:

Crafts Council
1 Oxenden Street
London SW1Y 4AT
Tel: 01 930 4811

Transport

Fuel duty rebate

The excise duty on the fuel used on local publicly available stage carriage bus services is rebated to operators by the Department of Transport.

For further information contact:

Department of Transport
Bus Licensing Division
2 Marsham Street
London SW1P 3EB
Tel: 01 276 4884

Rural bus grant

Recipients of the fuel duty rebate who operate in rural areas (outside urban areas with populations over 25,000) may be eligible for the rural bus grant. The grant is for 3.25p per eligible mile and is paid for four years. This scheme stops on 31 March 1990.

For further information contact:

Department of Transport
Bus Licensing Division
Room 59/18
2 Marsham Street
London SW1P 3EB
Tel: 01 212 4709

Railways and inland waterways freight facilities grant schemes

Grants of up to 60 per cent towards the capital cost of freight handling facilities are available for projects where road freight is transferred to rail or water, or where retaining freight on rail or water would be of significant environmental benefit to local communities.

Grants will be made only if such projects would not have gone ahead without such aid.

Further information can be obtained from:

Rail Freight Marketing Services Officer
British Railways Board
Euston House
24 Eversholt Street
London NW1 1DZ
Tel: 01 928 5151

Food, agriculture, horticulture, fisheries and woodlands

The following grant and assistance schemes of interest to small, growing businesses are operated by the Ministry of Agriculture, Fisheries and Food.

The Agricultural Assistance Scheme

The grants are paid on capital investments in agriculture and horticulture. A plan must be submitted showing that something new and with a life of at least ten years will be created, by the way of a first time project, replacement or an improvement. Investments in maintenance or to cover the cost of normal wear and tear are not allowed. The grant, which can cover between 15 and 60 per cent of costs, depending on the nature of the project, is also linked to the amount of labour employed or to be employed. The minimum expenditure that can be submitted under the Agricultural Assistance Scheme is £1,500 and the maximum is £35,000 per labour unit of 2,200 working hours per annum. Some conservation and horticultural projects attract a higher figure still.

To be eligible an applicant for this grant must:

(a) earn half or more of his or her annual income from agriculture;
(b) spend 1,100 or more hours per annum working in the agricultural field;
(c) hold an approved training certificate or have been a farmer for at least five years;

(d) not already be in receipt of a grant for an uncompleted development plan under one of the former agricultural development schemes;
(e) keep simple accounts for the life of the plan.

Under certain circumstances farmers under forty can be eligible for a supplement which increases the grant by a quarter.

Farm Diversification Grant Scheme (FDGS)

This scheme was launched in 1988 to assist existing agricultural businesses to develop alternative commercial uses for agricultural buildings and land. Eligible activities include good guality on-farm holiday accommodation, processing of farm produce and timber, craft manufacture and machinery repair, farm shops, sports and recreational facilities, educational and amenity facilities, livery and - in some areas only - facilities for hiring horses and ponies.

To be eligible an applicant must:

(a) have an established business and derive half or more of his or her income from agriculture and any eligible diversified farm business covered by the scheme;
(b) spend 1,000 or more hours per annum working in the agricultural field;
(c) hold an approved training certificate or have been in farming for at least five years.

The grant is in two parts with the minimum investment in the plan being £750. The maximum sum eligible for the grant is £35,000; however, applicants are not restricted as to their own investment level.

Enterprise feasibility studies

This is the first part of the grant scheme. It is intended to cover research work into project viability and to fund initial marketing costs.

Capital grants

This is a standard grant of 25 per cent throughout the UK on all eligible schemes. In general the grant will be available only if the scheme would otherwise not have gone ahead. Under certain circumstances farmers under forty can be eligible for an additional 25 per cent grant.

Futher information can be obtained from any local office of the Ministry of Agriculture, Fisheries and Food.

Food from Britain

Food from Britain has been established to provide farmers with help and advice in both forming co-operatives and applying for grant aid. The principal schemes in operation that it can advise on are the following.

Home Board

This is a programme of grants and other assistance to encourage small UK based businesses in the speciality (a term used to describe products with an 'individual', different, fine or country characteristic) food and drink sector to form voluntary groups and so expand or improve their operations.

Grant aid is available for feasibility studies, formation costs and some help with the cost of employing staff.

Agricultural and Horticultural Co-operative Grant Scheme

These grants are to help those involved in agriculture and horticulture to co-operate in marketing activities. Such co-operation must result in greater profit and efficiency:

1. *Capital grants* are available for between 25 and 30 per cent of the cost of buildings, works and certain items of equipment.
2. *Other grants* are available for research (up to 90 per cent), the formation of new co-operatives (up to 75 per cent) managerial salaries and expenses (up to 33.3 per cent for up to three years), training of managers (up to 75 per cent) and for surveys and studies to improve business efficiency (up to 75 per cent).

EC assistance

Grants are also available from the European Community towards the cost of substantial investment in the developing or improvement of processing or marketing of agricultural products.

Further information on these schemes can be obtained from:

Food from Britain
301–344 Market Towers
New Covent Garden Market
1 Nine Elms Lane
London SW8 5NQ
Tel: 01 720 2144

Forestry Commission

The Forestry Commission provides financial, professional and technical assistance to owners and prospective owners, or tenants, of woodlands.

The Woodland Grant Scheme

This scheme, announced in 1988, is intended to encourage the production of timber; provide jobs in rural areas; increase the economic potential of areas with declining agricultural populations; substitute for agricultural production in areas of surplus; enhance landscapes; create new habitats for wildlife; provide for long-term sport and recreational uses and to encourage conservation and regeneration of existing forest and woodlands. The grant can be between £615 and £1,775 per hectare.

The Farm Woodland Scheme

This scheme, also brought into effect in 1988, is intended to provide annual payments for up to forty years to help bridge the income gap between planting and obtaining the first income from thinning.

Further information can be obtained from:

The Forestry Commission
231 Corstophine Road
Edinburgh EH12 7AT
Tel: 031 334 0303

Fisheries

The Sea Fishing Authority

Can provide grants of up to £250,000 for the purchase of new vessels and any improvements made to them. Grants for improvements should demonstrate increased efficiency or economy in catching, handling, processing or storing fish or fish products; improved working conditions or improvements to the safety and seaworthiness of the vessel.

For further information contact:

Sea Fish Industry Authority
Sea Fish House
10 Young Street
Edinburgh EH2 4JQ
Tel: 031 225 2515

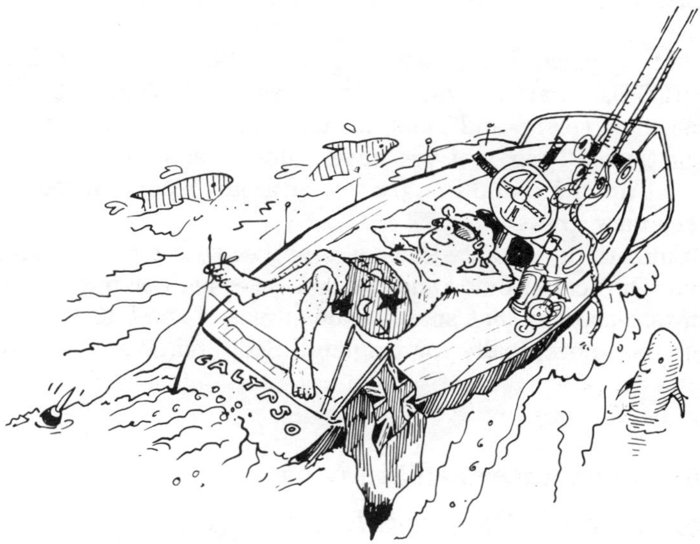

Highlands and Islands Development Board

Described in more detail in Section D: Scotland, the Board is able to provide financial assistance for fishery projects in Scotland. These projects can include the purchase of new or second-hand fishing vessels or projects dealing with such vessels or for boatyards, fishing farming, fish processing and other related industries.

For details contact the Board at the address given in Section D.

European Agricultural Guidance and Guarantee Fund (EAGGF)

The EAGGF provides a broad range of grant and other aid to those involved in the fishery business and in agriculture and food in general.

For details contact:

The Ministry of Agriculture,
Fisheries and Food
European and External Relations
Whitehall Place
London SW1A 2HH
Tel: 01 270 8000

B. REGIONAL ASSISTANCE

A number of organizations, including the Department of Trade and Industry (DTI), nationalized industries, development agencies, commissions, new towns and local authorities, have a hand in providing regional assistance. Their motives have much in common – to encourage business to set up or expand in a particular area – although their methods and resources vary greatly.

These organizations are listed below, together with a brief description of the assistance they can provide and the addresses and telephone numbers of contact points. Schemes that span various areas of the UK are listed first, followed by those specifically for England, Scotland, Wales and Northern Ireland.

Development and Intermediate Areas

The Department of Trade and Industry (DTI)

The government's regional assistance is spearheaded by the DTI, and concentrated into two categories of assisted area: Development Areas and Intermediate Areas. Slightly different forms of assistance are available in each area. The location of these is set out below. Northern Ireland, however, is treated quite differently, and this is explained at the end of this section.

The information given here is a summary only of each scheme. Detailed information can be obtained from the appropriate regional office of the DTI, whose addresses are given below.

Development Areas: England

North West Region

Liverpool
Widnes and Runcorn
Wigan and St Helens
Wirral and Chester
Workington

North East Region

Bishop Auckland
Hartlepool
Middlesbrough
Newcastle upon Tyne
South Tyneside
Stockton-on-Tees
Sunderland

East Midlands Region

Corby

South West Region

Falmouth
Helston
Newquay
Penzance and St Ives
Redruth and Camborne

Yorkshire and Humberside

Rotherham and Mexborough
Scunthorpe
Whitby

Development Areas: Scotland

Arbroath
Bathgate
Cumnock and Sanquhar
Dumbarton
Dundee
Glasgow
Greenock
Irvine
Kilmarnock
Lanarksire

Development Areas: Wales

Aberdare
Cardigan
Ebbw Vale and Abergavenny
Flint and Rhyl
Holyhead
Lampeter and Aberaeron
Merthyr and Rhymney
Neath and Port Talbot
Pontypridd and Rhondda
South Pembrokeshire
Wrexham

Intermediate Areas: England

North West Region

Accrington and Rossendale
Blackburn
Bolton and Bury
Manchester (part)
- Ashton-under-Lyne
- Audenshawe
- Cheetham Hill
- Davyhulme
- Denton
- Droylesden
- Dukinfield
- Eccles
- Failsworth
- Hulme
- Hyde
- Levenshulme
- Middleton
- Mossley
- Moss Side
- Moston
- Mottram in Longdendale
- Openshaw
- Prestwich
- Salford
- Stalybridge
- Swinton
- Trafford Park
- Weaste

Oldham
Rochdale

North East Region

Darlington
Durham
Morpeth and Ashington

Yorkshire and Humberside

Barnsley
Bradford
Doncaster
Grimsby
Hull
Sheffield

West Midlands Region

Birmingham
Coventry and Hinckley
Dudley and Sandwell
Kidderminster
Telford and Bridgnorth
Walsall
Wolverhampton

East Midlands Region

Gainsborough

South West Region

Bodmin and Liskeard
Bude
Cinderford and Ross-on-Wye
Plymouth

Intermediate Areas: Scotland

Ayr	Kirkaldy
Alloa	Lochaber
Badenoch	Newton Steward
Campbeltown	Skye and Wester Ross
Dunfermline	Stewartry
Dunon and Bute	Stranraer
Falkirk	Sutherland
Forres	Western Isles
Girvan	Wick
Invergordon and Dingwall	

Intermediate Areas: Wales

Bangor and Caernarvon	Newport
Bridgend	Pontypool and Cwmbran
Cardiff	Porthmadoc and Ffestiniog
Fishguard	Pwllheli
Haverfordwest	Swansea
Llanelli	

Regional Enterprise Grants

These grants are available to businesses in Development Areas with fewer than twenty-five employees, which must demonstrate, using a business plan, that both their ventures and the project in question are viable. Their new proposal must also lead to markets outside their immediate locality – so retailing, for example, is unlikely to be an acceptable area.

There are two types of grant.

Investment grants

Open to most manufacturing and some service sectors, the grant can be up to 15 per cent of expenditure on fixed assets, such as plant, machinery, buildings, land, site preparation and vehicles for use exclusively on site (e.g. fork lift trucks).

The maximum grant is £15,000.

Innovation grants

These will pay up to 50 per cent of eligible costs for projects which lead to the development and introduction of new products and processes. Such new products should have demonstrable improvements or advances on the company's present product range. Process development projects should lead to a significant increase in efficiency.

The maximum grant available is £25,000.

Regional Selective Assistance (RSA)

Businesses in assisted areas can apply for RSA, which is intended to encourage all industrial or commercial projects having a good chance of success. Such projects should create or safeguard employment; bring identifiable regional and national benefits, for example by improving productivity or increasing exports; and be unable to proceed without the support of RSA. Applicants will need to demonstrate that they can find most of the finance required themselves.

Project grant

The main form of RSA is tied to the number of jobs created or to the amount of fixed costs, such as purchase of land, site preparation and buildings, and plant and machinery (new and second-hand). Some non-recurring costs - patent applications, professional fees, instalation of machinery, for example - can also be funded in this way, as can increases in working capital. The amount of assistance given in this way is negotiable and will be the minimum necessary to allow the project to proceed as planned.

Some training grants, loan capital and exchange risk cover assistance are also available under RSA.

Contracts Preference Schemes

Businesses in Development Areas can apply for preferential treatment when tendering for contracts placed by government departments, nationalized industries and other public bodies.

Two preference schemes are operated.

The General Preference Scheme

This scheme gives businesses in the qualifying areas every opportunity to tender for public contracts for the supply of goods and services. Where price, quality, delivery and other considerations are equal government and public bodies will award contracts to businesses in the qualifying areas rather than elsewhere.

The Special Preference Scheme

This scheme is operated by government purchasing departments only. It can be applied when the lowest successful tenderer is located outside the qualifying areas. Provided the government department does not incur a greater cost, up to 25 per cent of the order can be given to a business within the qualifying area.

A booklet, Government Contracts Preference Schemes, is available from:

Department of Trade and Industry
Investment and Development Division
Bridge Place
88/89 Eccleston Square
London SW1 1PT
Tel: 01 215 7877

Industrial Expansion Teams

These DTI teams provide free confidential advice on locating in the assisted areas. They can offer a choice of suitable locations, arrange inspections and provide information on labour supply, transport, utilities and the general commercial and residential environment.

The Enterprise Initiative

Described earlier in Section A, this new initiative from the DTI, while applying across the UK, has additional benefits for businesses in assisted areas.

For further information contact one of the DTI offices whose address is given on the opposite page.

British Steel (Industry)

British Steel (Industry) — (BS(I)) — is a subsidiary of British Steel plc, established in 1975 to help businesses start up, expand, or relocate in nineteen designated areas of England, Scotland and Wales, where steel industry jobs have been lost.

The BS(I) areas are:

1. *Scotland* Lanarkshire, Cambuslang and S. E. Glasgow, Garnock Valley.
2. *England* Consett, West Cumbria, Derwentside, Hartlepool, Teesside, South Humber, Rotherham, Sheffield, Corby, Dudley.
3. *Wales* Deeside, Llanelli, West Glamorgan, Merthyr, Blaenau Gwent, South Glamorgan, South Gwent.

DTI offices

Location and selective financial assistance inquiries:

South West Industrial Development
Office
Phoenix House
Notte Street
Plymouth PL1 2HS
Tel. 0752 221891-5

England: general inquiries

Department of Trade and Industry
Bridge Place
88/89 Eccleston Square
London SW1V 1PT
Tel: 01 215 7877

England: regional offices

North East
Stanegate House
2 Groat Market
Newcastle upon Tyne NE1 1YN
Tel: 091 232 4722

North West
Sunley Tower
Piccadilly Plaza
Manchester M1 4BA
Tel: 061 236 2171

Yorkshire and Humberside
Priestley House
1 Park Row
Leeds LS1 5LF
Tel: 0532 443171

West Midlands
Ladywood House
Stephenson Street
Birmingham B2 4DT
Tel: 021 631 6181

East Midlands
Severns House
20 Middle Pavement
Nottingham NG1 7DW
Tel: 0602 506181

South East
Bridge Place
88/89 Eccleston Square
London SW1V 1PT
Tel: 01 215 7877

South West
The Pithay
Bristol BS1 2PB
Tel: 0272 272666

Scotland

Location advice:
Locate in Scotland
Scottish Development Agency
120 Bothwell Street
Glasgow G2 7JP
Tel: 041 248 2700

Industry Department for Scotland
Magnet House
59 Waterloo Street
Glasgow G2 7BT
Tel: 041 221 9833

Financial assistance inquiries:
Industry Dept for Scotland
Industrial Development Division
Alhambra House
45 Waterloo Street
Glasgow G2 6AT
Tel: 041 248 2855

Wales

Welsh Office
Industry Department
New Crown Building
Cathays Park
Cardiff CF1 3NQ
Tel: 0222 823 185

Northern Ireland

Belfast
Industrial Development Board for
Northern Ireland
IDB House
64 Chichester Street
Belfast BT1 4JX
Tel: 0232 233233

BS(I)'s assistance takes the forms discussed below.

Finance

BS(I) itself will provide finance where such help is necessary to enable a project to proceed.

The finance will be provided on attractive terms, and may be of the following types:

(a) unsecured loans for sums up to £25,000;
(b) secured loans up to £100,000;
(c) share capital, from £25,000, where this is more appropriate, often as part of a package which also includes loan finance;
(d) seed capital from its own funds, providing up to £10,000 of risk finance (usually very low interest loans with a share capital option) to help bring innovative projects to the point where commercial sources of finances can be obtained.

The Accelerated Business Development Scheme

This is designed to unlock the growth potential possessed by many established small businesses in the BS(I) areas. Under this scheme companies who have been trading for over three years, with annual turnover of up to £3 million, are eligible for a package of training and financial assistance.

Managed workshops for small enterprises

BS(I) operates 8 'Managed Workshops' complexes, providing more than 400 units for new small enterprises. These units range in size from a few hundred to few thousand square feet and are made available on a 3-monthly rolling licence agreement with the minimum of formalities. Business advice is freely available from the resident manager, and office services are also available.

Addresses of workshops

Blaenau Gwent	**Cardiff**
Unit 22 Pond Road Brynmawr Gwent NP3 4BL Tel: 0495 311625	Unit A Lewis Road East Moors Cardiff CF1 5EG Tel: 0222 471122

Corby
Central Works Site
Corby
Northants NN17 1YB
Tel: 0536 404215

Clyde
Fullarton Road
Tollcross
Glasgow G32 8YL
Tel: 041 641 4972

Coatbridge
Coatbank Way
Coatbridge
Lanarkshire ML5 3AG
Tel: 0236 23384

Hartlepool
Usworth Road Industrial Estate
Usworth Road
Hartlepool
Cleveland TS25 1PD
Tel: 0429 264128/235648

Normanby Park
Normanby Road
Scunthorpe
South Humberside DN15 8QZ
Tel: 0724 849457

Port Talbot
Addison Road
Port Talbot
West Glamorgan SA12 6HZ
Tel: 0639 887171

British Steel (Industry) contact points

Further information may be obtained from any of the offices listed below.

Head Office

British Steel (Industry) Ltd
Bridge House
Bridge Street
Sheffield
S3 8NS
Tel: 0742 731612

Regional Offices

London
Canterbury House
2–6 Sydenham Road
Croydon CR9 2LJ
Tel: 01 686 2311

Scotland
41 Oswald Street
Glasgow G1 1PA
Tel: 041 221 3372

North of England
Cleveland House
7 Woodlands Road
Middlesbrough
Cleveland TS1 3BH
Tel: 0642 244633

Wales and West Midlands
5th Floor,
Cleveland House
Clarence Place
Newport
Gwent NP9 7AA
Tel: 0633 244001

Yorkshire & Humberside
Bridge House
Bridge Street
Sheffield S3 8NS
Tel: 0742 700933

British Coal Enterprise

This was established in 1984 by the National Coal Board to increase job prospects and regenerate prosperity in the coalfield areas of Scotland, the North-East, the West, Yorkshire, Midlands, South Wales and the Midlands. Help is not limited to British Coal employees but the projects which it supports must result in permanent jobs being created in mining areas.

British Coal Enterprise can help almost anyone who has a proposal that will create real, new permanent jobs in mining areas: from a one-man operation, to big business – even international companies looking to expand and/or locate their operations in the coalfield areas of the UK.

The three major criteria are:

1. New permanent jobs must be created.
2. The project must be located in an area associated with coal mining.
3. The project must be financially viable.

British Coal Enterprise can help in five main ways, outlined below.

Advice and guidance

British Coal Enterprise knows the coalfield areas, the advisers, the business people, the financiers, the government bodies and the local councils in and around the areas extremely well. Positive links have been forged with enterprise agencies and it has encouraged the establishment of managed workshops in all coalfield areas.

Finance

Enterprise financial help is usually provided in the form of a loan. The amount of loan would, normally, be geared to the job creating element of the project (usually based on a figure of up to £5,000 for each new job created) and would normally not exceed 25 per cent of the total financial requirement of the project. Loans can be arranged relatively quickly, at favourable rates of interest, with few formalities, and, for small loans, usually without security. In addition to providing its own loans, the Enterprise can help put you in touch with other sources, e.g. DTI grants, local authorities, financial institutions, the private sector, the EC and enterprise agencies.

Premises

The Enterprise can help find suitable properties in coalfield areas for sale or to rent – at competitive prices. In some coalfield areas, buildings no longer needed by the coal industry may be available, and the Enterprise is also prepared to consider helping with the erection of new buildings in such coal mining areas for particular businesses. A number of ex-NCB premises and other buildings have been converted into managed workshops with great success, and this programme is continuing. A managed workshop provides smaller businesses and start-ups with workspace on an easy-in, easy-out basis at reasonable rentals and also provides on-site business advice and secretarial, reception, copying and other shared services.

Liaison with other forms and sources of help and advice

British Coal Enterprise also offers contacts with sources of other financial help, business advice, local expertise and government aid. By helping to cut through some of the red tape, Enterprise can save time, energy and money in relation to your business proposal.

Retraining

The Enterprise can identify and co-ordinate retraining programmes for those ex-employees leaving coal mining and seeking work in new companies.

Contact points

British Coal Enterprise has seven regional offices, which are responsible for activities in their localities:

Scotland
(Coalfield areas of Scotland)
Suite 1, Alloa Business Centre
The Whins
Alloa FK10 3SA
Tel: 0259 218021

Western
(Coalfield areas of north-west England, North Wales, Staffordshire, Shropshire and West Midlands (excluding Coventry))
Anderton House,
Lowton
Warrington
Cheshire WA3 2AG
Tel: 0942 672404

North East
(Coalfield areas of Northumberland, Tyne and Wear and Durham)
Gear House
Saltmeadows Road
Gateshead
Tyne & Wear NE8 3AH
Tel: 091 490 0866

Yorkshire
(Coalfield areas of Yorkshire)
Carcroft Enterprise Park
Station Road
Carcroft
Doncaster DN6 8DD
Tel: 0302 727228

Midlands
(Nottingham and the coalfield areas of Derbyshire, Leicestershire and Warwickshire)
Huthwaite
Sutton-in-Ashfield
Nottinghamshire NG17 2NP
Tel: 0623 554747

Enterprise House
Ashby Road
Coalville
Leicestershire LE6 2LA
Tel: 0530 813143

Kent
(Coalfield areas of Kent)
65 Burgate
Canterbury
Kent CT1 2HJ
Tel: 0227 761477

South Wales
East Moors Road
The Docks
Cardiff CF1 5EE
Tel: 0222 462667

European Regional Development Fund (ERDF)

The purpose of this scheme is to level out disparities in wealth between different regions in the European Community. The principal grant scheme operated by the ERDF of interest to small and growing businesses is the Business Improvement Services Scheme. Under this scheme grants of up to 70 per cent are available for manufacturing (except for steel, shipbuilding and textiles) and tourist and service projects (except for retailing and personal services).

Areas covered

Shipbuilding areas

Belfast, Cleveland, Merseyside, Strathclyde, Tyne and Wear

Steel areas

Cleveland, Clwyd, Corby, Durham Assisted Areas, Gwent, Humberside Assisted Areas, South Glamorgan, South Yorkshire including Sheffield, Strathclyde, Workington.

Textile areas

Greater Manchester
Aston-under-Lyne, Bolton, Bury, Leigh, Oldham, Rochdale and Wigan
Lancashire
Accrington, Blackburn, Burnley, Lancaster, Nelson and Rossendale
Northern Ireland
Tayside Assisted Areas
West Yorkshire
Bradford, Dewsbury, Halifax, Huddersfield, Keighley and Todmorden

Scotland

Similar schemes operate in Scotland. These are called Better Business Services or Better Technical Services, and informative leaflets covering all these schemes are available from regional offices of the DTI.

The grant

The grant covers such activities as:

1. *Marketing* – drawing up a strategy, exploring potential for products, and translation of sales literature:

2. *Management and financial advice* – for budget control systems and business plans and financial restructuring:

3. *New products and processes* – feasibility projects, licensing and translation:

4. *Computer applications and consultancy advice* – these grants are available to small and medium-sized enterprises employing up to 200 people. Twenty per cent grants towards the cost of fixed assets, including plant, buildings and machinery, to a maximum of £20,000, are also available to firms with up to twenty-five employees.

Under the scheme, providers of services to small firms in the eligible areas can receive grants for studies, risk appraisal, advice and counselling. Such providers can be from the private sector, local enterprise agencies, chambers of commerce, large firms interested in helping small firms, or local authorities depending on the service.

There is no limit to the number of services for which application can be made, although the DTI may restrict the total amount of grant help given to any one firm or organization.

Private individuals and organizations should apply to:

Department of Trade and Industry
Regional Policy and Development Grants Division
Kingsgate House
66–74 Victoria Street
London SW1E 6SW
Tel: 01 215 5000

C. ENGLAND

The Rural Development Commission

A statutory grant-in-aid body, the Commission has three main areas of activity, carried out within designated Rural Development Areas providing premises, helping small businesses and community development.

Premises

Providing small factories and workshops in rural areas ranging from a few hundred up to 5,000 square feet, is the Commission's principal activity. The Commission factories are constructed by English Estates, described later in this section.

In priority areas the Commission can provide grants of 25 per cent for converting redundant buildings into workshops.

Community development

The Commission can provide financial support for approved community and social projects. Its ACCORD (Assistance for Co-ordinated Rural Development) scheme launched in June 1987 can provide grants of up to 40 per cent of a project's start-up costs. ACCORD's objectives are:

1. To encourage new commercial opportunities that will lead to additional employment in rural communities.
2. To revitalize and strengthen the rural economy in those areas by encouraging increased investment and helping new businesses to get started.
3. To provide grants for initiatives which would not go ahead without help from the Commission, or that could go ahead but on a smaller scale.

All non-public organizations and individuals are eligible. ACCORD grants are most likely to be made available to projects involving business development, tourist attractions and recreational facilities; however other activities may also qualify if they help achieve the Commission's aims.

Help for small businesses

The Commission's aid to small businesses is provided through its Business Service – formerly the Council for Industries in Small Rural Areas (CoSIRA). These services are described in Chapter 1, Section C.

Further information on all the Commission's grants can be obtained from:

The Rural Development Commission
11 Cowley Street
London SW1P 3NA
Tel: 01 276 6969

English Estates

This is the trading name of the English Industrial Estates Corporation, a statutory body which develops and markets industrial and commercial property in England, both in the assisted and rural areas as well as elsewhere. Its principal services include the provision of:

(a) Beehive Workshops, which operate small workshop units from 500 square feet, let with full services on simple tenancy agreements at attractive weekly rentals;
(b) larger factories for manufacturing, service, warehousing or distribution companies;
(c) purpose-built units for high technology use, near to universities;
(d) a full professional design and build service for individual or specific property needs;
(e) a business support service for small and medium-sized businesses which are tenants or prospective tenants. Advice is given on all aspects of running a business, including start-up, expansion, marketing, finance and grants.

Further information can be obtained from any of the offices below:

Ashbourne
Millbank House
34 St John Street
Ashbourne
Derbyshire DE6 1GH
Tel: 0335 44616

Chatham
Pembroke
Chatham
Kent ME4 4UF
Tel: 0634 830010

Cockermouth
Lakeland Business Park
Cockermouth
Cumbria CA13 0QT
Tel: 0900 827161

Consett
No. 1 Industrial Estate
Medomsley Road
Consett DH8 6TY
Tel: 0207 590192

Doncaster
Hall Cross House
1 South Parade
Doncaster
South Yorks DN1 2DY
Tel: 0302 366865

Gateshead
Methven House
Kingsway
Team Valley
Gateshead
Tyne and Wear NE11 0LN
Tel: 091 4874711

Harrogate
10 North Park Road
Harrogate
North Yorks HG1 5PG
Tel: 0423 523024

Hereford
103/4 East Street
Hereford HR1 2LW
Tel: 0432 354331/2

Liverpool
Lancaster House
Mercury Court
Tithebarn Street
Liverpool L2 2QP
Tel: 051 236 3663

Manchester and North West
3rd Floor
75 Moseley Street
Manchester M2 3HR
Tel: 061 236 9550

Norwich
Bewick House
22 Thorpe Road
Norwich
Norfolk NR1 1RY
Tel: 0603 617006

Plymouth
5 Derriford Park
Derriford
Plymouth PL6 5QZ
Tel: 0752 795598

Sleaford
6 Carre Street
Sleaford
Lincolnshire NG34 7TW
Tel: 0529 306219

Thornaby
Forster House
Allensway
Thornaby
Stockton-on-Tees
Cleveland TS17 9HA
Tel: 0642 765911

Truro
Castle House
Pydar Street
Truro
Cornwall TR1 2UJ
Tel: 0872 40505

Yeovil
25 Hendford
Yeovil
Somerset BA20 1UN
Tel: 0935 29601

The Welsh and Scottish Development Agencies and the Local Enterprise Development Unit (LEDU) in Northern Ireland carry out a similar role in their respective areas. Details follow in the next two sections.

D. SCOTLAND

The Scottish Development Agency (SDA)

Established in December 1975, the SDA is responsible to the Secretary of State for Scotland and its aims are to promote economic development; provide, maintain and safeguard employment; promote industrial and international competitiveness; and to improve the environment. In pursuit of these aims, the SDA provides loans, gives guarantees and subscribes for equity or other shares in companies; establishes new enterprises alone or in partnership; constructs or lets specific need factories; and provides management advisory services.

Loans are arranged at competitive rates of interest with repayment terms up to twenty years. There is no upper limit to the amount available to a business, but security is normally required. Small businesses employing up to 100 people who require amounts up to £50,000 are handled by the Agency's Small Business Division. The SDA also looks after the European Coal and Steel Community funds in Scotland (see Chapter 5, Section D: 'Government and EC financing schemes'. The following schemes are operated by the SDA.

LEG-UP (Local Enterprise Grants for Urban Projects)

This scheme provides up to 50 per cent towards the cost of fixed assets for urban projects in Scotland that will make a positive contribution to the environment or create jobs. Awards are made quarterly on a competitive basis and commercial residential, industrial and leisure projects are all eligible.

PRIDE (Programme for Rural Initiative Development)

This scheme extends to most rural areas of Scotland many of the benefits urban areas receive from LEG-UP. Assistance towards the cost of fixed assets - land, building, machinery, etc. - can be considered if they meet PRIDE's general aims and it can be shown that the project could not go forward without its help. A business plan will be needed and private funds should amount to two and a half times the sum which PRIDE puts up.

DRAW (Development of Rural Area Workshops)

Aimed at rural areas with a population of less than 15,000 outside the area covered by the Highlands and Islands Development Board, assistance is available to small businesses seeking either their first workshop or planning to expand, and to property owners wishing to convert an existing building for this purpose.

Premises

The SDA performs in Scotland a similar service to English Estates, building and managing factories from 500 to over 100,000 square feet. These are available on rental, long leases or for outright purchase.

Advisory services

The SDA provides a full range of general business counselling services, has training facilities and offers advice on marketing and export. Through the

Business Development Scotland Scheme, advice and consultancy are available to the larger Scottish companies looking for help with diversification, market appraisal and business planning.

Further information is available from:

Small Firms Service
21 Bothwell Street
Glasgow G26 NR
Tel: 041 248 6014
Freefone Enterprise

SDA centres

Centres to contact are:

Aberdeen
Aberdeen Office
Queen's Road
Aberdeen AB1 6YT
Tel: 0224 641791

Coatbridge
Unit 33
Coatbridge Business Park
204 Main Street
Coatbridge ML5 3RB
Tel: 0236 24371

Dundee
Dundee Project Office
Nethergate Centre
Yeaman Shore
Dundee DD1 4BU
Tel: 0382 29122

Dumfries
Business Development Centre
16 Buccleuch Street
Dumfries DG1 5AH
Tel: 0387 54444

Edinburgh
Rosebery House
Haymarket Terrace
Edinburgh EH12 5EZ
Tel: 031 337 9595

Galashiels
Small Business Division
Wheatland Road
Galashiels TD1 2HQ
Tel: 0896 58991

Glasgow
East End Business Centre
Parkhead Library
64 Tollcross Road
Glasgow G31 4XA
Tel: 041 556 7412

Hillington
Merlin House
Morseland Road
Hillington
Glasgow G52 4XY
Tel: 041 882 6288

Inverclyde
Project Office
64/66 West Blackhall Street
Greenock PA15 1XG
Tel: 0475 24533

Kirkcaldy
441 High Street
Kirkcaldy KY1 2SX
Tel: 0592 205171

Motherwell
Project Office
28 Brandon Parade
Motherwell ML1 1UJ
Tel: 0698 54626

Newhouse
Newhouse Industrial Estate
Rowantree Avenue
Motherwell ML1 5RX
Tel: 0698 732637

Stirling
Alpha Centre
Stirling University Innovation Park
Stirling FK9 4NF
Tel: 0786 70080

Highlands and Islands Development Board (HIDB)

The HIDB began its operations in November 1965 with the objective of assisting the people of the Highlands and Islands to improve their economic and social conditions. Its work covers an area above the 'Highland Line', embracing almost half the mass of Scotland but less than 7 per cent of the population. It works very closely with the SDA.

The HIDB offers a wide range of special incentives to manufacturing or process industry, craft, tourist facilities, fisheries, agriculture, and some categories of service industry. Assistance can be by way of grants, interest-free loans for buildings, plant, equipment and working capital. The HIDB can also hold shares.

The level of grant and loan assistance available would not normally be greater than 50 per cent but in exceptional cases it can go up to 70 per cent.

The HIDB also builds factories to lease to developers, and provides advisory services in general management, finance, personnel, production, distribution and marketing.

For further information contact:

The Highlands and Islands
Development Board
Bridge House
20 Bridge Street
Inverness IV1 1QR
Tel: 0463 234171

E. WALES

Welsh Development Agency (WDA)

The WDA became operative on 1 January 1976 and carries out a similar role in Wales to that carried out in Scotland by the Scottish Development Agency. It helps new businesses to settle in Wales and existing enterprises to expand through funding and property packages tailored to individual needs.

Financial assistance

The WDA's investment funds are provided in the form of equity capital or fixed-rate loans. The WDA will subscribe for up to 30 per cent of the equity of any company and is prepared to negotiate buy-back arrangements. Its five- to ten-year loans are provided at competitive fixed interest rates and security is required. Small businesses which plan to create new jobs in rural locations can obtain loans at about 3 per cent below current commercial lending rates. The WDA can also arrange low-cost loans through European Coal and Steel Community funds, for job creation in areas affected by the run-down of coal and steel.

The Business Development Unit

The Business Development Unit offers a range of support programmes for small businesses. It has a team of advisers who have many years' experience of the private sector and small businesses. They are able to help companies identify their immediate and longer-term requirements, provide up-to-date advice and information on a wide range of business matters including business planning, management accounting, training, premises, finance and grants. It also has a team of specialist advisers in the area of marketing and production.

There is also a facility where individuals contemplating setting up in business can, in an open-plan environment, license a range of plant and equipment in the areas of metalworking, woodworking, joinery and garment manufacture in order to develop ideas and products before setting up on their own account.

The Business Development Unit is also responsible for the Small Firms Service in Wales and its team of some sixty experienced business counsellors are available to give practical advice to inquirers. There is a range of courses available to those contemplating self-employment as well as certain specialized courses for events both in the UK and overseas, and it is responsible for the administration of the funded consultancy element of the DTI's Enterprise Initiative.

It can be contacted at:

Business Development Centre
Treforest Industrial Estate
Pontypridd
Mid Glam CF37 5UT
Tel: 0443 841777

WDA Head Office and regional offices

Head Office
Pearl House
Greyfriars Road
Cardiff CF1 3XX
Tel: 0222 222666

North West Wales
Llys Garth
Garth Road
Bangor
Gwynedd LL57 2RT
Tel: 0248 370082

North East Wales
Wrexham Industrial Estate
Wrexham
Clwyd LL13 9UF
Tel: 0978 661011

West Wales
Cillefwr Industrial Estate
Johnstown
Camarthen
Dyfed SA31 3RB
Tel: 0267 235642

South Wales (East)
1 & 2 Gold Tops
Newport
Gwent NP9 4YW
Tel: 0633 244666

South Wales (West)
Swansea Industrial Estate
Fforestfach
Swansea
West Glam
SA5 4DL
Tel: 0792 561666

Bridgend Industrial Estate
Bridgend
Mid Glam
CF31 3SD
Tel: 0656 656531

South Wales (Valleys)
Treforest Industrial Estate
Pontypridd
Mid Glam CF37 5UT
Tel: 0443 841131

Hirwaun Industrial Estate
Nr Aberdare
Mid Glam CF44 9UU
Tel: 0685 811268

Mid Wales Development

Mid Wales Development (formerly the Development Board for Rural Wales) offers factories, finance, business advice and other services to encourage enterprises to locate and expand in Caredigion in Dyfed, Meisonnydd in Gwynedd and the three districts of Brecknock, Montgomery and Radnor in Powys.

Its services include the following.

Finance

A full range of financial assistance is available including its own version of Regional Selective Assistance: the Mid Wales Development Grant. A subsidized loan facility is also available.

Premises

Units from 750 to 20,000 square feet are available on most sites, and larger ones can be built on demand. Costs start at around £2 per square foot including rates, and concessions (on rent and rates) are available in certain areas.

Other services

These include the Business Advisory Service, providing a comprehensive range of help and advice; trade fairs and exhibitions at home and abroad; and a meetings and exhibition centre in London's West End.

Further details may be obtained from:

Mid Wales Development
Ladywell House
Newtown
Powys SY16 1YB
Tel: 0686 626965
Freephone 0800 269300

WINvest

Established in 1983 by bringing together the inward investment activity of the Welsh Office Industry Department, the Welsh Development Agency and the former Development Corporation for Wales, WINvest provides a 'one stop' contact point for any potential industrial investor. The organization operates as a division of the Welsh Development Agency, and its services are free and confidential.

Further details can be obtained from:

WINvest
Pearl Houses
Greyfriars Road
Cardiff CF1 3XX
Tel: 0222 223666

F. NORTHERN IRELAND

Extensive powers exist to help industry to set up, operate and expand in Northern Ireland. Most measures are aimed primarily at manufacturing industries, but job-creating service industries may be eligible.

Standard assistance

This is offered without regard to the number of jobs created.

Key Worker grants

Substantial grants are available for transferring key workers into Northern Ireland, including fares, removal expenses, a contribution towards lodgings, and legal and other fees in connection with the purchase of a house.

Rates relief

Premises classified as industrial in Northern Ireland are totally exempt from rates.

Other grants

Training grants and Management Development Programme grants are available for personnel at various levels – see Chapter 4, Section A, subsection 'Training in Northern Ireland' for further details.

Selective assistance

Special assistance can be negotiated for projects which are especially attractive because of the number of jobs created, particularly if those jobs are in areas of high unemployment, or because they help the economy by, for example, introducing the manufacture of new products. Employment can be created either in new projects or in the expansion of existing ones. The assistance available can include the following.

Capital grants

Up to 50 per cent of the cost of new buildings, machinery and equipment can be made available.

Employment grants

These are related to the number of newly created jobs and designed to provide new projects with an inflow of revenue during the build-up period.

Rent relief

Up to 100 per cent relief for up to five years is available, irrespective of whether the premises are government or privately owned.

Interest relief grants

These grants can be made available to reduce the interest on loans from non-government sources. Relief can be granted for up to seven years: three years at a broadly commercial rate followed by four years at 3 per cent per annum.

Management incentive grants

These are available in certain circumstances to help a company attract and recruit good quality management.

Loans

Various forms of equity participation and loans can be made available.

Research and development

These grants are available mainly to the manufacturing or processing industries and provide up to a maximum of 50 per cent of the first £50,000 of eligible costs and 40 per cent of eligible cost above that, with a top level of grant of £250,000 for any single project.

These rates are applicable to work done in Northern Ireland only. Work done in Britain or abroad and work done by consultants from outside Northern Ireland will be limited to a lesser grant rate of 25 per cent.

Market Development Grant Scheme

The scheme helps local firms financially to develop a strategic approach to their marketing, planning and implementation. It helps firms to develop a logical step-by-step approach to marketing and is available either as a

package, or as individual components to help improve marketing practices within overall operations.

The components of the package are planning, marketing audit, marketing plan, implementation, sales aids, packaging, test marketing, staff reallocation, customer visits, recruitment, fairs and exhibitions.

The title of the scheme is the 40/30 Plan, and firms embarking on such a programme may apply for assistance amounting to 40 per cent of approved costs up to a maximum of £30,000 per year.

The Local Enterprise Development Unit (LEDU)

This small business agency can help manufacturing, craft or service businesses which employ up to fifty people. Its Product Ideas Licensing Library can help you to find a start-up area, or its Research and Development Grant Scheme can help you to bring your own product to market. It maintains a register of private and public property and can provide technical advice on a wide range of matters.

The Local Enterprise
Development Unit (LEDU)
25–27 Franklin Street
Belfast BT2 8BT
Tel: Freefone LEDU (only in
Ireland)
0232 242582

The LEDU's business centre in Linenhall Street has been specially designed to hold trade shows, and is available for small businessmen to mount their own exhibitions. A counselling service is operated and four local area offices are keen to assist. All can be contacted on the Freefone number.

Area offices

For all offices: Tel: Freefone LEDU

East
17/19 Linenhall Street
Belfast BT2 8AA

North
13 Ship Quay Street
Londonderry BT48 6DJ

South
6–7 The Mall
Newry
Co Down BT34 1BX

West
15 High Street
Omagh BT8 1BA

Further information on all the schemes in this section and on all forms of assistance available in Northern Ireland may be obtained from:

Industrial Development Board
for Northern Ireland
IDB House
64 Chichester Street
Belfast BT1 4JX
Tel: 0232 233233

G. LOCAL AUTHORITIES AND OTHER LOCAL INITIATIVES

As well as the regional assistance described in the previous sections, an extensive range of grant aid and other help for new and growing businesses is available from local authorities. Some of these are listed below. However, this field is in a constant state of evolution, so contact the organization referred to, to keep up to date.

Local financial assistance?

Pros

- Grants provide free money
- Subsidized loans save you money
- You can borrow money against grants and in this way 'gear-up' your investment

Cons

- You might be tempted to move to a part of the country that does not suit you or your business
- You might be tempted to borrow too much money against grants you receive
- You might be tempted to borrow too much money, even at subsidized rates

General powers

Under a number of Acts of Parliament local authorities in England, Scotland and Wales have certain general powers which they can use to help industry, where their interests and those of businessmen coincide. Many councils are also enterprise agency sponsors. Some examples of local authority aid are given below.

Hammersmith and Fulham

This local authority has a setting-up grant for new businesses moving into their first business premises. On presentation of a business plan showing the venture's viability a grant of up to £5,000 can be given. Grants or loans are also available for building improvements, ethnic minority ventures, market research, technology consultancy and training.

Greenwich

The London Borough of Greenwich can invest up to £30,000 in any local business.

Cornwall

Cornwall provides start-up loans of £3,000 or bank guarantees up to £10,000.

Devon

Devon has established its own venture capital fund to make investments in local businesses in the range £50,000–250,000.

You should contact your local council's Industrial Development Officer, located in the Chief Executive's Department, for details of schemes and help in your area.

City Grant

This grant, of between £200,000 and £400,000, will be paid direct by the government to private sector developers for reclamation, new buildings or refurbishment projects in inner-city areas which provide jobs or private housing; bring derelict lands and empty buildings back into use; improve the local environment and help rebuild confidence in inner-city areas.

Further information can be obtained from any regional office of the Department of the Environment on this grant and on others such as those covering derelict land and the Urban Programme for Environmental Improvements.

Inner urban areas

Under the Inner Urban Areas Act 1978, local authorities for the Designated Areas, listed below, have the power to:

(a) declare 'improvement areas' in which they can give grants or make loans for environmental improvements and the conversion and improvement of industrial or commercial buildings;
(b) make loans of up to 90 per cent for up to thirty years, on commercial terms, for the acquisition and development of land, the work on which must be of benefit to the inner-city area;
(c) provide loans and grants of up to £1,000 towards the administration and other set-up costs associated with forming a co-operative.

The Act also provides further powers for use within defined areas within the Designated Areas, known as 'special areas'. These are:

(a) grants to help with rents for businesses taking on new leases;
(b) two-year interest-free loans for site preparation;
(c) interest relief grants for loans on land and buildings, to small firms employing fewer than fifty people.

Designated Areas

England

Barnsley
Birmingham
Blackburn
Bolton
Bradford
Brent
Bristol
Burnley
Coventry
Derby
Doncaster
Dudley
Gateshead
Greenwich
Hackney
Halton
Hammersmith and Fulham
Haringey
Hartlepool
Islington
Kensington and Chelsea
Kingston upon Hull
Kirklees
Knowsley
Lambeth
Langbaurgh
Leeds
Leicester
Lewisham
Liverpool
Manchester
Middlesbrough
Newcastle upon Tyne
Newham
North Tyneside
Nottingham
Oldham
Plymouth
Preston
Rochdale
Rotherham
St Helens
Salford
Sandwell
Sefton
Sheffield
South Tyneside
Southwark
Stockton-on-Tees
Sunderland
Tower Hamlets
Walsall
Wandsworth
Wigan
Wirral
Wolverhampton
Wrekin

Scotland

City of Dundee
City of Glasgow
Clydebank
Dumbarton
Hamilton
Inverclyde
Monklands
Motherwell
Renfrew

Wales

Afan
Blaenau Gwent
Cardiff
Cynon Valley
Merthyr Tydfil
Newport
Ogwr
Rhondda
Rhymney
Swansea

Enterprise Zones

Enterprise Zones have been defined within some inner cities and other neglected urban black spots. The zones can give new businesses substantial financial benefits as well as freedom from control. In this way business both inside and on the perimeter of the zones will be strengthened. The zones are not aimed exclusively at small or new firms, but nevertheless they provide an attractive commercial inducement to locate in them. The first zone to become operational was in the lower Swansea Valley, in June 1981, and the last was north-west Kent.

The facilities, grants and other assistance available within each zone are comprehensively described in a booklet.

The booklet is available from:

The Department of the Environment
2 Marsham Street
London SW1P 3EB
Tel: 01 276 3000

In summary these measures are:

1. One hundred per cent capital allowances (for corporation and income tax purposes) for commercial and industrial buildings.
2. Exemption from general rates on industrial and commercial property.
3. Simplified planning procedures.
4. Exemption from Industrial Training Board levy and the provision of information.
5. Quicker handling of requests for customs warehousing and inward processing relief and a relaxation of criteria applying to 'private' customs warehouses.
6. A reduction to the minimum of the requirement to supply statistical information to the government.

Local contact points

England

Corby
Director of Industry
Corby Development Centre
Grosvenor House
George Street
Corby
Northants NN17 1TZ
Tel: 0536 62571

Dudley
Economic Development Unit
7 St James Road
Dudley
West Midlands DY1 1HP
Tel: 0384 456000

Glanford
Glanford Borough Council
Council Offices
Station Road
Brigg
South Humberside DN20 8EG
Tel: 0652 52441

Hartlepool
Economic Development Officer
Civic Centre
Hartlepool
Cleveland TS24 8AY
Tel: 0429 266522

London (Isle of Dogs)
London Docklands Development Corporation
Enterprise House
41 Millharbour
London E14 9XX
Tel: 01 515 3000

Middlesbrough
Department of Economic Development
Vancouver House
Gurney Street
Middlesbrough
Cleveland TS1 1QP
Tel: 0642 222279

North West Kent
NW Kent EZ Office
Civic Centre
Strood
Rochester
Kent ME2 4AW
Tel: 0634 732716/727777

Rotherham
Rotherham Metropolitan Borough Council
Department of Planning
Norfolk House
Walker Place
Rotherham
South Yorkshire S60 1QT
Tel: 0709 372099

Salford
Administrative and Industrial Liaison Officer
City of Salford
Civic Centre
Chorley Road
Swinton
Greater Manchester M27 2AD
Tel: 061 793 3403/061 794 4711

Scunthorpe
Scunthorpe Borough Council
Civic Centre
Ashby Road
Scunthorpe
South Humberside DN16 1AB
Tel: 0724 280444

Speke
City Estate Surveyor's Department
Liverpool City Council
Municipal Buildings
Dale Street
Liverpool L69 2DH
Tel: 051 285 3640

Telford
Telford Development Corporation
Newtown House
Telford Square
Telford
Shropshire TF3 4JS
Tel: 0952 293131

Trafford
Trafford Park Development Corporation
Trafford Wharf Road
Trafford Park
Manchester N17 1EX
Tel: 061 848 8000

Tyneside (Gateshead)
Gateshead Metropolitan Borough Council
Civic Centre
Gateshead
Tyne and Wear NE8 1HH
Tel: 091 477 1011

Tyneside (Newcastle)
Newcastle City Council Services
Civic Centre
Newcastle upon Tyne NE1 8QN
Tel: 091 232 8520

Wakefield
Economic Development Department
Estates and Valuation Section
City of Wakefield Metropolitan District Council
Bishopsgarth
Wakefield
West Yorks SF1 3RA
Tel: 0924 290900

Wellingborough
Director of Development
Wellingborough Borough Council
Croyland Hall
Burystead Place
Wellingborough
Northants NN8 1AH
Tel: 0933 228885

Workington
Economic Development Officer
Town Hall
Oxford Street
Workington
Cumbria CA14 2PT
Tel: 0900 604351

Scotland

Clydebank
Scottish Development Agency
120 Bothwell Street
Glasgow G2 7JF
Tel: 041 248 2700

Invergordon
Highlands and Islands Development Board
62 High Street
Invergordon IV18 0DH
Rosshire
Tel: 0349 853666

Tayside (Arbroath)
Director of Planning
Angus District Council
County Buildings
Market Street
Forfar DD8 3LG
Tel: 0307 65101

Tayside (Dundee)
Dundee Project Office
Nethergate Centre
Yeaman Shore
Dundee DD1 3BU
Tel: 0382 29122

Wales

Delyn
Delyn Borough Council
Delyn House
Aber Park
Flint
Clwyd CH6 5BD
Tel: 03526 62345

Lower Swansea Valley
Director of Planning
Swansea City Council
The Guildhall
Swansea SA1 4PE
Tel: 0792 302946

Milford Haven Waterway
Pier House
Pier Road
Pembroke Dock
Dyfed SA72 6TR
Tel: 0646 684914

Northern Ireland

Belfast
Belfast Enterprise Zone Office
9–21 Adelaide Street
Belfast BT2 8NR
Tel: 0232 248449

Londonderry
Londonderry Enterprise Zone Office
Richmond Chambers
The Diamond
Londonderry BT48 6HN
Tel: 0504 263992

New towns

These towns were set up under the New Towns Act 1959 and their role was further amended by the New Towns and Urban Development Corporation Act 1985.

These towns are able to offer new and developing businesses special aid on top of any other government or local government assistance for which they are eligible – to induce them to locate in their area.

They mostly have workspace, factory and in some cases retail premises let on flexible 'easy come, easy go' leases. Some offer rent-free periods of up to two years as an inducement, as well as packages of loans, grants, training and business advice.

For further general information contact:

Commission for the New Towns
Glen House
Stag Place
London SW1E 5AJ
Tel: 01 828 7722

Scottish New Towns
17–19 Cockspur Street
London SW1Y 5BL
Tel: 01 839 2117

Ulster Office
Industrial Board for Northern Ireland
11 Berkeley Street
London W1X 6BU
Tel: 01 493 0601

New Town Commission and Development Corporation addresses

For further specific information contact:

England

Basildon
Basildon Commission for the New Towns
Gifford House
London Road
Bower Gifford
Basildon
Essex SS13 2EX
Tel: 0268 553261

Bracknell
Commission for the New Towns
Glen House
Stag Place
London SW1E 5AJ
Tel: 01 828 7722

Central Lancashire
Central Lancashire Commission for the New Towns
Cuerden Pavilion
Shady Lane
Bamber Bridge
Preston
Lancashire PR5 6AZ
Tel: 0772 38211

Corby
Corby Commission for the New Towns
Chisholm House
9 Queen's Square
Corby
Northants NN17 1PA
Tel: 0536 203535

Crawley
Commission for the New Towns
Glen House
Stag Place
London SW1E 5AJ
Tel: 01 828 7722

Harlow
Commission for the New Towns
Glen House
Stag Place
London SW1E 5AJ
Tel: 01 828 7722

Hatfield
Commission for the New Towns
Glen House
Stag Place
London SW1E 5AJ
Tel: 01 828 7722

Hemel Hempstead
Commission for the New Towns
Glen House
Stag Place
London SW1E 5AJ
Tel: 01 828 7722

Milton Keynes
Milton Keynes Development Corporation
Saxon Court
502 Avebury Boulevard
Central Milton Keynes MK9 3HS
Tel: 0908 692692

Northampton
Northampton Commission for the New Towns
2–3 Market Square
Northampton NN1 1PA
Tel: 0604 29966

Peterborough
Peterborough Commission for the New Towns
PO Box 3
Stuart House
City Road
Peterborough PE1 1UJ
Tel: 0733 68931

Peterlee
Aycliffe and Peterlee Investment Company Ltd
St Cuthbert's House
Durham Way North
Aycliffe Industrial Estate
Newton Aycliffe
Co Durham DL5 6AW
Tel: 0325 300808

Redditch
Redditch Commission for the New Towns
Highfield House
Headless Cross Drive
Redditch
Worcs B97 5EU
Tel: 0527 401100

Skelmersdale
Skelmersdale Commission for the New Towns
High Street
Pennylands
Skelmersdale
Lancs WN8 8AR
Tel: 0695 24242

Telford
Telford Development Corporation
Newtown House
Telford Square
Telford TF3 4JS
Tel: 0952 293131

Warrington and Runcorn
Warrington and Runcorn Commission for New Towns
PO Box 49
New Town House
Buttermarket Street
Warrington
Cheshire WA1 2LF
Tel: 0925 51144

Washington
Washington Commission for New Towns
Usworth Hall
Stephenson
District 12
Washington
Tyne and Wear NE37 1AP
Tel: 091 416 3591

Welwyn Garden City
Commission for the New Towns
Glen House
Stag Place
London SW1E 5AJ
Tel: 01 828 7722

Northern Ireland

Ballymena
Department of the Environment
Northern Division
43 Thomas St
Ballymena BT43 6BA
Tel: 0266 653655

Craigavon
Craigavon Enterprise Centre
Carn Industrial Estate
Portadown
Craigavon
Co. Armagh BT63 5RH
Tel: 0762 333393

Londonderry
Londonderry Development Corporation
Richmond Chambers
The Diamond
Londonderry BT48 6HN
Tel: 0504 260734

Scotland

Cumbernauld
Cumbernauld Development Corporation
Cumbernauld House
Cumbernauld
Scotland G67 3JH
Tel: 02367 21155

East Kilbride
East Kilbride Development Corporation
Atholl House
East Kilbride
Scotland G74 1LU
Tel: 03552 41111

Glenrothes
Glenrothes Development Corporation
Unicorn House
Falklands Place
Glenrothes
Scotland KY7 5PD
Tel: 0592 754343

Irvine
Irvine Development Corporation
Perceton House
Irvine
Ayrshire KA11 2AL
Tel: 0294 214100

Livingston
Livingston Development Corporation
Sidlaw House
Almondvale
Livingston
West Lothian
Scotland EH54 6QA
Tel: 0506 414177

Wales

The Development Board for Rural Wales
Ladywell House
Newtown
Powys SY16 1JB
Tel: 0686 26965

Cwmbran
Cwmbran Development Corporation
Gwent House
Town Centre
Cwmbran
Gwent NP4 3XJ
Tel: 06333 67777

Urban development corporations

These have been established by the government to regenerate their areas in such a way as to attract new investment and development. They have powers to provide loans and grants towards the assembly and reclamation of land, infrastructure provision and environmental improvements.

Seven corporations are fully operational and a further four (Bristol, Leeds, Central Manchester and Sheffield) are being established.

Further information may be obtained from:

Department of the Environment
2 Marsham Street
London SW1P 3EB
Tel: 01 276 3000

Welsh Office
Cathays Park
Cardiff CF1 3NQ
Tel: 0222 823175

or from the corporations, whose addresses are given overleaf.

Addresses of the corporations

Black Country Development Corporation
Round Green Road
Oldbury
West Midlands B69 2DG
Tel: 021 511 2000

Cardiff Bay Development Corporation
Baltic House
Mount Stuart Square
Cardiff CF1 6DH
Tel: 0222 471576

London Docklands Development Corporation
Enterprise House
41 Millharbour
London E14 9XX
Tel: 01 515 3000

Teesside Development Corporation
Tees House
High Force Road
Riverside Park
Middlesbrough
Cleveland TS2 1RE
Tel: 0642 230636

Trafford Park Development Corporation
Waterside
Trafford Wharf Road
Trafford Park
Manchester M17 1EX
Tel: 061 848 8000

Tyne and Wear Development Corporation
Hadrian House
Higham Place
Newcastle upon Tyne NE1 8AF
Tel: 091 222 1222

Merseyside Development Corporation
Fourth Floor
Royal Liver Building
Pier Head
Liverpool L3 1JH
Tel: 051 236 6090

Industrial development associations

A number of English regions have industrial development associations sponsored by the Department of Trade and Industry, to provide a range of financial aid, advice and preliminary marketing information, to help businesses locate in their area.

Information on their various services can be obtained from:

Devon and Cornwall Development Bureau
Derriford Business Park
Derriford
Plymouth PL6 5QZ
Tel: 0752 793379

INWARD (Agency for Investment into North West England)
Duxbury Park
Duxbury Hall Road
Chorley PR7 4AT
Tel: 02572 69626

Northern Development Company
Bank House
Carliol Square
Newcastle upon Tyne NE1 6XE
Tel: 091 261 0026

Yorkshire and Humberside Development Association
Westgate House
100 Wellington Street
Leeds LS1 4LT
Tel: 0532 439222

West Midlands Industrial
Development Association
Chantry House
High Street
Coleshill
West Midlands B46 3BP
Tel: 0675 62577

Enterprise Boards

These are development companies established by local authorities to provide a focus for their many activities to encourage and assist enterprise development in their area.

The Boards can often provide loan and venture capital, management consultancy and advice, training and management development and help with property development.

The Boards are:

Greater London Enterprise Board
63–67 Newington Causeway
London SE1 6BD
Tel: 01 403 0300

Lancashire Enterprise PLC
Enterprise House
17 Ribblesdale Place
Preston PR1 3NA
Tel: 0772 203020

West Midlands Enterprise Board
Wellington House
31–34 Waterloo Street
Birmingham B2 5TJ
Tel: 021 236 8855

West Yorkshire Enterprise Board
First Floor, Elizabeth House
9–17 Queen Street
Leeds LS1 2TW
Tel: 0532 420505

Freeports

Sometimes referred to as Free Zones, Freeports are the result of an attempt by the government made in 1984 to emulate the entrepreneurial havens of the Far East. Three of the six UK Freeports are based on airports (Belfast, Prestwick, Birmingham) and three on seaports (Liverpool, Cardiff and Southampton).

The Freeports allow users to process, store and manufacture goods without paying customs duties and local taxes. Goods can then be exported without these duties being paid, with obvious cash flow advantages to anyone in the re-export field.

For further information contact your local Customs and Excise department office.

4 Training

When you invest in training you are investing in the single most important commodity in business – people. In the coming years the business world will face rapid changes in the economy, demanding new skills, and we are warned that people will become increasingly more difficult to recruit in the 1990s as the labour market feels the effect of the falling birth rate. This has been referred to as 'the demographical time-bomb'. Training not only improves the skills and efficiency of your workforce, it also motivates them to remain with you.

There is also evidence that management training for the owner–manager of a smaller firm can significantly reduce the chance of failing and, indeed, improve the performance of the business. No formal academic qualifications are required for most courses and costs are generally modest. They take a variety of forms, varying between one-day topic courses covering areas like selling skills, bookkeeping, computers, financial management, etc,. through to longer courses of fifteen days spread over six months (the Firmstart programme in Business Growth Training). They are frequently run at weekends and sometimes on evenings during the week. There is also The Small Business Programme, a distance learning programme, which allows you to improve your management skills in your own home and at your own pace.

Why bother with training?

Pros
- Improves your firm's performance
- Reduces your chance of failure
- Allows you to learn from the experience of others
- Represents a permanent investment in yourself and your workforce
- Enables you to compete more effectively with other firms

Cons
- It takes time and can cost money
- You might not be able to spare the time when the course is being run
- You will have to travel to the course
- You may not like 'formal learning'
- You may have confidential business information you do not wish to disclose

A. SUBSIDIES FOR TRAINING IN SMALL BUSINESS

New Entrant Training Scheme (NETS)

For businesses employing less than twenty people in eligible areas, NETS is aimed at people under nineteen already employed by the firm, and it provides them with a series of one-week training sessions over a one- to three-year period. The costs are subsidized.

For information contact:

The Rural Development Commission
141 Castle Street
Salisbury
Wiltshire SP1 3TP
Tel: 0722 336255

Extra skill training

Eligibility criteria as for NETS, this scheme is for proprietors or employees who need extra skills, usually in the production/manufacturing field. The scheme comprises intensive two- to five-day courses.

For information contact the Rural Development Commission (address above).

New technology skills

A training grant of up to 40 per cent, matched by a further grant of 40 per cent from the European Social Fund is available to businesses located in an Assisted Areas (see Chapter 3, Section B: Regional assistance).

The assistance is available towards the cost of training people under twenty-five in skills associated with new technology. Each trainee should receive at least 200 hours of training over a period no longer than three years. The grant is not available for normal replacement training or for ongoing training.

For further information contact the appropriate regional office of the Department of Trade and Industry, listed in Chapter 3, Section B under the Enterprise Initiative.

Training in Northern Ireland

Extensive powers exist to help industry in Northern Ireland with training. These include the following.

Training grants

Such grants are available for training personnel at various levels.

Key Worker grants

Substantial grants are available for transferring key workers from anywhere outside Northern Ireland. These grants may cover free fares (including preliminary visit), plus a contribution towards lodgings, household removal expenses and legal and other fees in connection with the purchase of a house.

Training centres

Free instruction for selected workers and assistance in training company supervisors and instructors are both available.

Rates relief

Premises classified as industrial for rating purposes in Northern Ireland are totally exempt from rates.

Management Development Programme

This offers three types of grant aid to companies engaged in manufacturing or selected service sectors:

1. *Consultant Grant Scheme* – 50 per cent of the fees, £1,000 is maximum receivable, of employing a management consultant to identify the company's management training needs.
2. *Training Grant Scheme* – 50 per cent of the fees for external management training courses or for an external trainer to deliver an in-company course.
3. *Trainee Manager Development Scheme* – 50 per cent of the salary, £6,000 is maximum receivable of a newly recruited management trainee aged under thirty.

For further information contact:

Industrial Development Board
for Northern Ireland
IDB House
64 Chichester Street
Belfast BT1 4JX
Tel: 0232 233233

European Social Fund (ESF) training schemes

ESF is primarily an employment, training and retraining fund. Its purposes are to improve employment opportunities for workers, notably by increasing their geographical and occupational mobility, and to soften the impact of technological change. Finance is directed to those regions or groups of workers judged to be in greatest need.

Within the UK the guidelines include Northern Ireland as an absolute priority area, and certain areas suffering from changes in the steel, shipbuilding, textile and fishing industries, and areas of high and long-term unemployment. The areas covered are listed below.

Travel to work areas: England

North/North East	*North West*
Alnwick and Amble	Accrington and Rossendale
Bishop Auckland	Blackburn
Darlington	Bolton and Bury
Durham	Burnley
Hartlepool	Liverpool
Middlesborough	Manchester
Morpeth and Ashington	Oldham
Newcastle Upon Tyne	Pendle
South Tyneside	Rochdale
Stockton-on-Tees	Widnes and Runcorn
Sunderland	Wigan and St Helens
	Wirral and Chester

East

Barnsley
Bradford
Castleford and Pontefract
Chesterfield
Doncaster
Gainsborough
Goole & Selby (Humberside part, i.e. Goole)
Grimsby
Hull
Mansfield
Nottingham (City UPA only)
Retford
Worksop
Scunthorpe
Sheffield (South Yorks part only)
Wakefield and Dewsbury
Worksop

West Midlands

Birmingham (excluding Hereford & Worcester part)
Coventry and Hinckley (excluding Leicestershire part, ie Hinckley)
Dudley and Sandwell (excluding Hereford & Worcester and Staffordshire parts)
Telford and Bridgnorth
Walsall
Wolverhampton

Travel to work areas: Scotland

Eastern

Alloa
Arbroath
Bathgate
Dundee
Dunfermline
Falkirk
Kirkcaldy
Stirling*

Western

Ayr
Cumnock & Sanquhar
Dumbarton
Girvan
Glasgow
Greenock
Irvine
Kilmarnock
Lanarkshire

Travel to work areas: Wales

Clwyd

Flint and Rhyl
Wrexham

Dyfed

Llanelli
Swansea (part)

Mid Glamorgan

All

South Glamorgan

Cardiff (part)

West Glamorgan

All

Gwent

Ebbw Vale & Abergavenny (part)
Merthyr & Rhymney (part)
Newport
Pontypool & Cwmbran

Powys

Aberdare (part)
Ebbw Vale & Abergavenny (part)
Swansea (part)

Eligible Schemes

The European Social Fund will match money given to schemes by public authorities such as local authorities and Government Departments. In general, the level of support available is between 50% of the total running costs of the scheme and 25% of the money given by the public authority. Elements of costs which the Fund will contribute are:

Trainee Allowances
Scheme Preparation
General Running Expenses
Scheme Management
Vocational Guidance
Training Assessment
Subsistence and Travel
Wage Subsidies Paid to Employers.

Contact addresses

These are:

Department of Employment
European Social Fund Unit
6th Floor
11 Belgrave Road
London SW1V 1RB
Tel: 01 834 6644

Department of Economic Development
EC Branch
Arches Centre
11–13 Bloomfield Avenue
Belfast BT5 5HD
Tel: 0232 732411

B. BUSINESS GROWTH TRAINING (BGT)

The largest provider of training for the owner–managers of smaller firms is the Training Agency (formerly the Manpower Services Commission). In 1989 it relaunched the range of training and consultancy programmes it runs as part of Business Growth Training. BGT offers five options, which cover developing a training plan, developing better business skills, managing change and developing innovative training solutions to meet new challenges.

Option 1

This is a free kit which covers writing or revising your business plan and financial forecasts and then looking at the people in your business and matching them to the skills you need, to produce a training plan. The kit is available from local authorized agents. You can obtain their names from your local area office of the Training Agency (listed at the end of this section).

Option 2

This covers the business training of owner-managers. Four programmes are offered by the Training Agency. Subsidized fees are charged for each programme.

The Small Business Programme

This is a modular, distance learning programme developed at a cost of £1.5 million. It is designed for growing firms and is based on modules comprising video tape, audio tape and workbook, supported by locally organized workshops and *The Small Business Programme Handbook*. It is structured around activities designed to address the typical problems faced by a growing firm.

For full details contact .

The Small Business Programme
Cranfield School of Management
Cranfield
Bedford MK43 0AL
Tel: 0234 750414/751122

The Small Business Programme Handbook

To obtain copies of the Handbook, contact your local bookseller or :

Paul Chapman Publishing Ltd
144 Liverpool Road
London N1 1LA
Tel: 01 609 5315/6

Private Enterprise Programme (PEP)

These are a series of one-day topic-based seminars on subjects like marketing, finance and administration. You can obtain a list of courses from your local area office of the Training Agency (listed at the end of this section).

Firmstart

This is a practical training programme for owner–managers who have just set up in business. It is part time, at weekends and evenings, with fifteen training days spread over six months. In addition, participants are allocated a counsellor to work with. Participants are expected to produce a business plan as part of the programme. The programme is run throughout the UK with various start dates.

Contact one of the following for details:

North East
Durham University Business School
Durham DH1 3LB
Tel: 091 374 2000

North West
Manchester Business School
Booth Street West
Manchester M15 6PB
Tel: 061 275 6333

East Midlands
Nottingham Polytechnic
Business Development Centre
Burton Street
Nottingham NG1 4BU
Tel: 0602 418418

West Midlands
Warwick Business School
University of Warwick
Coventury CV4 7AL
Tel: 0203 523523

East and North London
Cranfield School of Management
Cranfield
Beds MK43 0AL
Tel: 0234 751122

London and South East
London Business School
Sussex Place
Regent's Park
London NW1 4SA
Tel: 01 262 5050

West
Enterprise Unit
University of Bristol
Wills Memorial Building
Queen's Road
Bristol BS8 1HR
Tel: 0272 303615

South West
Dorset Institute
Holland House
Oxford Road
Bournemouth BH8 8EZ
Tel: 0202 298626/28

Scotland
Scottish Enterprise Foundation
University of Stirling
Stirling FK9 4LA
Tel: 0786 73171

Growth programmes

These are programmes for managers of growing firms. They vary in length and structure but are generally similar to Firmstart – part time at weekends and evenings. Participants are allocated a counsellor to work with. Programmes are run throughout the UK with various start dates. Generally they are run by the same organizations running Firmstart. However, you obtain the address of other providers from your local area office of the Training Agency (listed at the end of this section).

Option 3

This provides half the cost (up to a maximum of £15,000) of working with a consultant to review your business strategy and develop and implement a training plan for your firm. The project may last for up to a year. You can obtain the addresses of approved consultants from your local area office of the Training Agency (listed below).

Option 4

This provides up to half the cost (up to a maximum of £100,000) of a group of companies undertaking a survey of training needs, and developing and implementing joint training courses. This option can also be used by established employer groups such as local chambers of commerce.

Option 5

This provides free training specialists, and possibly financial support, to help design innovative training programmes for particular companies.

Details of the five BGT options are available from area offices of the Training Agency, listed in the following subsection.

Training Agency area offices

London Region

Inner London North
1st Floor, 236 Grays Inn Road
London WC1 8HL
Tel: 01 827 3311

Inner London South
200 Great Dover Street
London SE1 4YB
Tel: 01 357 7110

London East
3rd Floor, Cityside House
40 Adler Street
London E1 1EW
Tel: 01 377 1866

London North
6th Floor, 19–29 Woburn Place
London WC1 0LU
Tel: 01 837 1288

London South
Skyline House
200 Union Street
London SE1 0LX
Tel: 01 928 0800

London West
Lyric House
149 Hammersmith Road
London W14 0QL
Tel: 01 602 7227

East Midlands and Eastern Region

Bedfordshire and Cambridgeshire
1st and 2nd Floors, Wesley House
19 Chapel Street
Luton LU1 2SE
Tel: 0582 412828

Derbyshire
4th Floor, St Peter's House
Gower Street
Derby DE1 1SB
Tel: 0332 290550

Leicestershire and Northamptonshire
1st Floor, Rutland Centre
Halford Street
Leicester LE1 1TQ
Tel: 0533 538616

Lincolnshire
5th Floor, Wigford House
Brayford Wharf
Lincoln LN5 7AY
Tel: 0522 532266

Norfolk and Suffolk
Crown House
Crown Street
Ipswich
Suffolk IP1 3HS
Tel: 0473 218951

Nottinghamshire
4th Floor, Lambert House
Talbot Street
Nottingham NG1 5GL
Tel: 0602 413313

West Midlands Region

Birmingham and Solihull
15th and 16th Floors, Metropolitan House
1 Hagley Road
Birmingham B16 8TG
Tel: 021 456 1199

Coventry and Warwickshire
5th and 6th Floors, Bankfield House
163 New Union Street
Coventry CV1 2QQ
Tel: 0203 631133

Dudley and Sandwell
6th Floor, Falcon House
The Minories
Dudley DY2 8PG
Tel: 0384 455391

Staffordshire
Moorlands House
Trinity Street
Hanley
Stoke on Trent ST1 5LN
Tel: 0782 262131

The Marches, Hereford/Worcester
2nd Floor, Hazledene House
Central Square
Telford TF3 4JJ
Tel: 0952 291471

Wolverhampton and Walsall
2nd Floor, 30 Market Street
Wolverhampton WV1 3AF
Tel: 0902 311111

Northern Region

Cleveland
Corporation House
73 Albert Road
Middlesbrough
Cleveland TS1 2RU
Tel: 0642 231023

County Durham
Valley Street North
Darlington
Co Durham DL1 1TJ
Tel: 0325 351166

Northumberland and North Tyneside
Welbar House Gallowgate
Newcastle upon Tyne NE1 4TD
Tel: 091 232 6181

Sunderland
South Tyneside and Gateshead
Derwent House
Washington New Town
Tyne and Wear NE38 7ST
Tel: 091 416 6161

North West Region

Cheshire
1st Floor, Spencer House
Dewhurst Road
Birchwood Centre
Warrington WA3 7PP
Tel: 0925 826515

Cumbria
1st and 2nd Floors, Thirlmere Building
50 Lakes Road
Derwent Howe
Workington CA14 3YP
Tel: 0900 66991

Lancashire
3rd Floor, Duchy House
96 Lancaster Road
Preston PR1 1HE
Tel: 0772 203077

Central Manchester
4th and 5th Floors, Boulton House
17–21 Chorlton Street
Manchester M1 3HY
Tel: 061 236 7222

Greater Manchester North
Bayley House
St George's Square
Bolton BL1 1HB
Tel: 0204 397350

Manchester East
1st Floor, 1 St Peter's Square
Stockport SK1 1NN
Tel: 061 477 8830

Merseyside
3rd Floor, Tithebarn House
Tithebarn Street
Liverpool L2 2NZ
Tel: 051 236 0026

South West Region

Avon
PO Box 164
4th Floor, Minister House
27 Baldwin Street
Bristol BS99 7HR
Tel: 0272 277116

Devon and Cornwall
7th Floor, Intercity House
Plymouth Station
Plymouth
Devon PL4 6AA
Tel: 0752 671671

Dorset and Somerset
Crescent House
The Mount
Taunton
Somerset TA1 3TT
Tel: 0823 259121

Gloucestershire and Wiltshire
Conway House
33–35 Worcester Street
Gloucester GL1 3AJ
Tel: 0452 24488

South East Region

Berkshire and Oxfordshire
5th Floor, Kings Point
120 Kings Road
Reading
Berks RG1 3BZ
Tel: 0734 586262

Buckinghamshire and Hertfordshire
2nd Floor, 31 Octagon Parade
High Wycombe
Bucks HP11 2LD
Tel 0494 33473

Essex
Globe House
New Street
Chelmsford
Essex CM1 1UG
Tel: 0245 358548

Hampshire and Isle of Wight
25 Thackeray Mall
Fareham Shopping Centre
Fareham
Hants PO16 0PQ
Tel: 0329 285921

Kent
5th Floor, Mountbatten House
28 Military Road
Chatham
Kent ME4 4JE
Tel: 0634 44411

Surrey
Technology House
48–54 Goldsworth Road
Woking
Surrey GU21 1LE
Tel: 0486 228190

Sussex
Gresham House
12–24 Station Road
Crawley
West Sussex RH10 1HT
Tel: 0293 562922

Yorkshire and Humberside Region

Bradford, Calderdale and Kirklees
5th Floor, Provincial House
Tyrell Street
Bradford BD1 5NW
Tel: 0274 723711

Humberside
4th Floor, Essex House
Manor Street
Hull HU1 1YA
Tel: 0482 226491

North Yorkshire and Leeds
Fairfax House
Merrion Street
Leeds LS2 8JU
Tel: 0532 446181

Sheffield and Rotherham
8th Floor, Sheaf House
The Pennine Centre
Hawley Street
Sheffield S1 3GA
Tel: 0742 701911

Wakefield, Doncaster and Barnsley
York House
31–36 York Place
Leeds LS1 2EB
Tel: 0532 450502

Scotland

Ayrshire, Dumfries and Galloway
25 Bank Street
Kilmarnock KA1 1ER
Tel: 0563 44044

Central and Fife
5 Kirk Loan
Corstrophine
Edinburgh EH12 7HD
Tel: 031 334 9821

Glasgow City
4th Floor, George House
36 North Hanover Street
Glasgow G1 2AD
Tel: 041 552 3411

Grampian and Tayside
Argyll House
Marketgait
Dundee DD1 1UD
Tel: 0382 29971

Highlands and Islands
3rd Floor, Metropolitan House
31–33 High Street
Inverness IV1 1TX
Tel: 0463 220555

Lanarkshire
106 Park St
Crosshill Street
Motherwell ML1 1PF
Tel: 0698 51411

Lothian and Borders
Orchard Brae House
30 Queensferry Road
Edinburgh EH4 2HS
Tel: 031 315 2888

Renfrewshire, Dumbarton and Argyll
5 Elm Bank Gardens
Charing Cross
Glasgow G2 4PN
Tel: 041 226 5544

Wales

Dyfed and West Glamorgan
3rd Floor, Orchard House
Orchard Street
Swansea SA1 5AP
Tel: 0792 460355

Gwent
Government Building
Cardiff Road
Newport
Gwent NP9 1YE
Tel: 0633 815697

Gwynedd, Clwyd and Powys
Wynnstay Block
Hightown Barracks
Kingsmill Road
Wrexham LL13 8BH
Tel: 0978 290333

Mid and South Glamorgan
5th Floor, Phase One Building
Ty Glas Road
Llanishen
Cardiff CF4 5PJ
Tel: 0222 755744

C. TRAINING BOARDS

There are some industry sectors that have their own Training Boards.

Construction Industry Training Board

The Board has introduced a three-day residential programme for potential and existing proprietors of small firms. It covers: marketing, working with people, safety, estimating, planning and organizing and financial management. It also has a very comprehensive catalogue of training publications and audio-visual aids.

Further information may be obtained from:

Construction Industry Training Board
Bircham Newton
King's Lynn
Norfolk PE31 6RH
Tel: 0553 776677

Dewhurst House
24–30 West Smithfield
London EC1A 9JA
Tel: 01 489 1662

Hotel and Catering Training Company

The Company runs frequent short courses for people starting up in these industries. It also offers a small business service from regional centres around the country.

Further information can be obtained from:

Hotel and Catering Training Company
International House
High Street
Ealing
London W5 5DB
Tel: 01 579 2400

Agricultural Training Board

The Agricultural Training Board (ATB) makes payments to the following:

(a) groups of farmers and growers formed as formally constituted associations registered with the ATB for the organization of training carried out in conformity with agreed programmes;
(b) employers of trainees over eighteen who registered in the Agricultural and Horticultural Training Scheme after 1 April 1984, towards associated further education course expenses.

Further information including details of current rates and conditions may be obtained from:

Agricultural Training Board
46 London Road
Reading
RG1 5AF
Tel: 0734 864643

Other Training Boards

The following Training Boards may also have subsidized training schemes for small business.

Clothing and Allied Products Industry Training Board
80 Richardshaw Lane
Pudsey
Leeds
LS28 6BN
Tel: 0532 393355

Engineering Industry Training Board
P.O. Box 176
54 Clarendon Road
Watford
Herts
WD1 1LB
Tel: 0923 38441

Offshore Petroleum Industry Training Board
Forties Road
Montrose
Angus
Scotland DD10 9ET
Tel: 0674 72230

Plastics Processing Industry Training Board
Coppice House
Halesfield 7
Telford
Shropshire
TF7 4NA
Tel: 0952 587020

Road Transport Industry Training Board
Capitol House
Empire Way
Wembley HA9 0NG
Tel: 01 902 8880

D. BUSINESS EDUCATION INITIATIVE

To help all sectors of business to work more closely with the education system at all levels, the Department of Trade and Industry (DTI) has a number of initatives.

The Teaching Company Scheme

The DTI and the Science and Engineering Research Council can provide financial help to universities and polytechnics to place young graduates in firms planning major operational changes. The firms make a financial contribution and in return gain professional help backed up by the resources of the local college.

Regional technology centres

These centres have been established by the DTI and enable universities and colleges in an area to feed in information about their research and development sources, consultancy services and training opportunities. Firms can find out easily what is available in their own region.

Working with schools

The DTI can arrange to introduce firms to people and organizations who can help them become more actively involved with schools. This will help employers develop links with schools and help them to become actively involved with curriculum development, school management and the promotion of enterprise activites in educational establishments.

For further information, contact regional offices of the DTI, listed in Chapter 3, Section B: Regional assistance.

E. PICKUP

Professional, industrial and commercial updating – this is a programme designed by the Department of Education and Science (DES) to encourage educational institutions to help businessmen and women and their employees to keep up with the latest technology and skills.

The PICKUP scheme is operated in colleges, universities and polytechnics and can take any form: one-to-one tutorials, distance learning, small group work and form lectures.

Teaching can take place at an education centre, at the workplace or at home - and at different times of the day, week or year. For small firms the scheme can offer individual teaching or can bring together several businesses with the same or similar needs. PICKUP provision can cover any facet of general business, or it can be tailored to the needs of a particular industry or employer.

Each course comprises four days' full-time tuition for a group of ten students, spread over a period of six weeks. Courses are not free - they must cover their costs - and the DES says that owner-managers should expect to pay a realistic price for training. More details of courses and costs are available from the PICKUP agents.

Where to go for a PICKUP

As well as a national centre in London, the PICKUP scheme is operated locally by regional agents.

The contacts are:

National PICKUP
Adult Training Promotions Unit
Department of Education and Science
Elizabeth House
York Road
London SE1 7PH
Tel: 01 934 0888

Bedfordshire, Cambridgeshire, Essex, Hertfordshire, Norfolk, Suffolk
Tel: 0223 421075

Cheshire, Lancashire, Manchester, Merseyside
Tel: 02572 75474

Derbyshire, Leicestershire, Lincolnshire, Northamptonshire, Nottinghamshire
Tel: 0602 298298

Hereford, Worcester, Shropshire, Staffordshire, Warwickshire, West Midlands
Tel: 0902 714771

Avon, Cornwall, Devon, Dorset, Gloucestershire, Somerset, Wiltshire
Tel: 0272 659075

Berkshire, Buckinghamshire, NW London, Oxfordshire
Tel: 0990 27417
Tel: 0990 27418

Cleveland, Cumbria, Durham, Northumberland, Tyne and Wear
Tel: 091 261 0851

East Sussex, Hampshire, Isle of Wight, Kent, Surrey, West Sussex
Tel: 0784 439050

Humberside, North Yorkshire, South Yorkshire, West Yorkshire
Tel: 0532 438634

Scotland
Tel: 031 244 5426

Wales
Tel: 0443 493696

F. YOUTH SELF-EMPLOYMENT OPPORTUNITIES

Enterprise scholarships

These are open to university or college students showing outstanding ability or insight into the area of business enterprise. The scholarships are to allow them to develop relevant knowledge and practical skills while at college.

> *Details may be obtained from:*
>
> Scottish Enterprise Foundation
> University of Stirling
> Stirling FK 9 4LA
> Tel: 0786 73171

Workface

Face offers training places to young people under the Training Commission's Youth Training Scheme. As well as providing the opportunity to learn a skill, it provides help to those who want to set up in business for themselves. This support and guidance can continue for up to three years after the training period has finished.

> *The address is:*
>
> Workface
> Market Place
> Glastonbury
> Somerset BA6 9HL
> Tel: 0458 33917

Fairbridge/YES (Youth Enterprise Scheme)

With assets of £6 million this organization can provide 'soft loans' (i.e. loans at subsidized rates or over extended periods) of up to £5,000 – applicants must be able to back their own project too.

Information may be obtained from:

Fairbridge/YES
Victoria Chambers
16–20 Strutton Street
London SW1P 2HP
Tel: 01 222 3341

Graduate Enterprise Programme

This programme is established to help recent graduates of universities and colleges to set up their own businesses. An intensive foundation course, continuous counselling, a training allowance and a market research grant all combine to make this an unbeatable package for potential new entrepreneurs.

The programme is run throughout the UK with various start dates between July and September.

Contact one of the following for details:

North East
Graduate Into Enterprise
Durham University Business School
Durham DH1 3LB
Tel: 091 374 2000

North West
Manchester Business School
Booth Street West
Manchester M15 6PB
Tel: 061 275 6333

East
Cranfield School of Management
Cranfield
Beds MK43 0AL
Tel: 0234 751122

West Midlands
Warwick Business School
University of Warwick
Coventry CV4 7AL
Tel: 0203 523523

London and South East
South East England Consortium
PO Box 501
1 Water Lane
London E15 4LU
Tel: 01 319 3568

South West
Eterprise Unit
University of Bristol
Wills Memorial Building
Queen's Rd
Bristol BS8 1HR
Tel: 0272 303615

Yorks and Humberside
Dept of Economic and Marketing Studies
Huddersfield Polytechnic
Queen's Gate
Huddersfield HD1 3DH
Tel: 0484 22288

Wales
Enterprise Institute
Cardiff Business School
Aberconway Building
Colum Drive
Cardiff CF1 3EU
Tel: 0222 874000

Scotland
Scottish Enterprise Foundation
University of Stirling
Stirling FK9 4LA
Tel: 0786 73171

Graduate Gateway

This is a programme to help unemployed graduates to develop small business skills. They work in a 'consultancy' role in a small business for three months, and are certainly better prepared to start their own firm after their experience. A training allowance is paid throughout (Also at Durham University Business School and Bath University).

Details are obtainable from:

Graduate Gateway
University of Glasgow
25 Bute Gardens
Glasgow G12
Tel: 041 339 8855

Headstart

This is a national Industrial Society project, which is run in centres all over the country. It is a free eight-week training programme comprising 120 hours of training, for anyone wishing to start their own business.

Further information can be obtained from:

The Industrial Society
48 Bryanston Square
London W1H 7LH
Tel: 01 839 4300

Live Wire

This scheme helps young people aged sixteen to twenty-five to get their own business started. Run all over the UK as a competition, with the winners receiving good four-figure prizes and everyone securing help and advice. The initiative comes from Shell UK, but it has many other supporters.

Information may be obtained from:

Live Wire
60 Grainger Street
Newcastle upon Tyne NE1 5JG
Tel: 091 261 5584

National Youth Enterprise Centre

The Centre aims to act as a national resource centre for information, publication, training, research and development, and as a forum for association, discussion and joint action in the broad field of the social education of young people.

Contact:

National Youth Enterprise Centre
17–23 Albion Street
Leicester LE1 6GD
Tel: 0533 471200

The Prince's Youth Business Trust

The Trust helps eighteen- to twenty-five-year-olds with a viable business idea to get started. It provides grants of up to £15,000 and loans of up to £5000. To be considered you need to present a business plan – but the Trust can help you to put one together. Its advisers provide support and encouragement to all recipients for at least a year after the money is put in.

Further details may be obtained from:

The Prince's Youth Business Trust
8th Floor, Melbury House
Melbury Terrace
London NW1 6LZ
Tel: 01 262 1340

5 Obtaining Finance

Obtaining finance is never easy, or so it seems. The Governor of the Bank of England, however, has claimed that there is plenty of money for the right sort of investment. The problem seems to be that there are different types of money - loan and equity capital - and you need to know what you are looking for and where it can be found. This is certainly an area where any small-business person needs professional advice.

Most small firms finance the bulk of their expansion from funds generated by the business itself. The problem is that you may have to wait a long time before you have sufficient funds to operate in this way. By then that lucrative business opportunity could have disappeared.

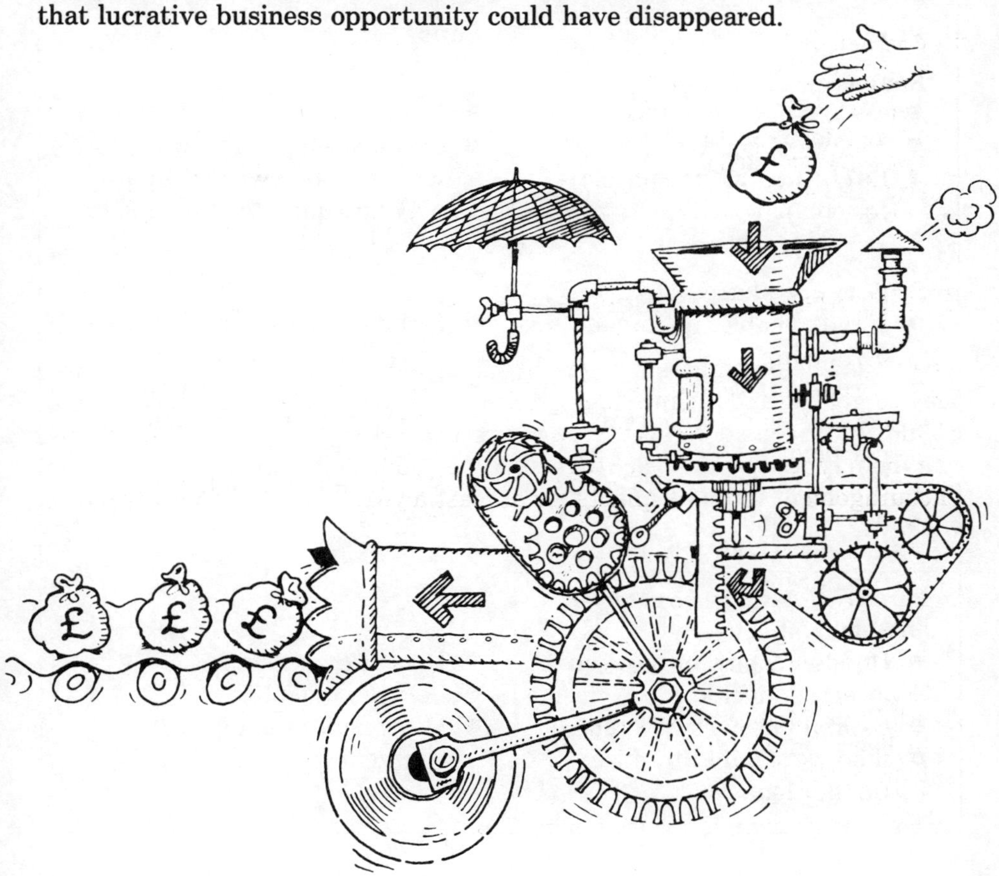

First you have to decide how much you need and when you will need it. This entails drawing up a proper financial budget, in particular a cash flow forecast. Indeed, if you are seeking outside funds you will need to include these in a proper business plan that gives details of how you intend to make the most of that business opportunity and achieve the budgeted financial results you hope for. The business plan is an important document. You cannot hope to obtain any sort of finance without it.

Once you know how much you need, you must decide what form that finance should take. It could be debt or equity finance or even matched borrowing like factoring or leasing. Every business needs to have an adequate equity base of risk capital. This allows you to 'gear-up' with debt finance such as overdrafts or term loans. Equity and debt need to be carefully balanced to match the risks the business is likely to face.

How should I finance my business?

Pros	Cons
Loans	
• No loss of ownership • No loss of control • Interest is tax deductible for company	• Interest *must* be paid • Capital repayments *must* be met . . . otherwise company may be liquidated and assets seized
Preference shares	
• If redeemable, no loss of ownership • If redeemable, no loss of control unless dividends not paid • If convertible, capital need not be repaid • Increases ability to raise further loans	• If redeemable, capital must be repaid • If convertible you may lose both ownership and control at some future date • May result in a higher tax charge
Ordinary shares	
• Dividends paid only when directors decide • Capital not normally repaid • Increases ability to raise further loans	• Loss of ownership • Loss of control • May result in a higher tax charge

A. LOANS

Loans form the mainstay of external funds used by small firms. There are a number of different types of loans.

1. *Overdrafts* – which are available as a facility on your current account but must be repaid on demand. These are relatively cheap because you pay interest only on the amount you overdraw but are risky because they may be recalled by the bank at any time. You pay interest at a certain rate above bank base rate.
2. *Short-term loans* – are available for periods between one and five years. They may be fixed rates of interest or at a certain rate above bank base rate (called variable).
3. *Long-term loans* – are available for periods over five years. They may be at fixed or variable rates of interest.

Often you have to provide security to obtain a loan. This might take the form of a 'charge' on your business or personal assets or, a personal guarantee.

The major provider of loans are the clearing banks.

Clearing banks

Clearing – or High Street – banks offer a wide range of services in their own right. Through wholly or partly owned subsidiaries they cover virtually every aspect of the financial market. Their services include overdrafts, term loans, trade bill finance, factoring, leasing, export and import finance, the Government Loan Guarantee Scheme, and equity financing in some cases.

In addition to providing a source of funds, the clearing banks have considerable expertise in the areas of tax, insurance and financial advice generally.

Table 5.1 lists the principal UK clearing banks and summarises their small business services.

Table 5.1 UK clearing banks and their small business services

Bank	SBS	GLGS	VC	FS
Allied Irish Banks		●		
Bank of Ireland		●		
Bank of Scotland		●	●	
Barclays Bank	●	●	●	●
Clydesdale Bank*		●	●	●
Co-operative Bank	●	●		
Girobank	●	●		
Lloyds Bank	●	●	●	●
Midland Bank	●	●		●
National Westminster Bank	●	●	●	●
Northern Bank*		●		
Royal Bank of Scotland		●		●
Ulster Bank†	●	●		
Yorkshire Bank		●		

Notes: SBS = Small Business Section
GLGS = Government Loan Guarantee Scheme
VC = Venture capital
FS = Franchise Section
* Member of Midland Bank Group
† Member of NatWest Group

Principal UK clearing banks

Addresses for the banks listed in Table 5.1 are as follows:

Allied Irish Banks Ltd
Bankcentre-Britain
Bellmonte Road
UXBRIDGE UB8 1SA
Tel: 0895 72222

Bank of Ireland
36 Queens Street
LONDON EC4R 1BN
Tel: 01 329 4500 x512

Bank of Scotland
2 Robertson Avenue
EDINBURGH
EH11 1PZ
Tel: 031 346 6051

Barclays Bank plc
Chatsworth House
66–70 St Mary Axe
LONDON EC3 A8BD
Tel: 01 283 2033

Clydesdale Bank plc
Business Dev. Unit-Retail
30 St Vincent Place
GLASGOW
G1 2HL
Tel: 041 248 7070

Co-operative Bank plc
P.O. Box 101
1 Balloon Street
MANCHESTER M60 4EP
Tel: 061 832 3456

Girobank plc
101 Pentonville Road
LONDON N1 9XR
Tel: 01 833 8111

Lloyds Bank plc
Head Office
7 Lombard Street
LONDON
EC3P 3BS
Tel: 01 626 1500

Midland Bank plc
Small Business Unit
Griffin House
Pennine Centre
41 Silver Street Head
SHEFFIELD S2 3GG
Tel: 01 260 8000

National Westminster Bank plc
Small Business Services
8 Fenchurch Place
LONDON EC3M 4PB
Tel: 01 374 3374

Northern Bank Ltd
P.O. Box 183
Donegall Square West
BELFAST BT1 6JS
Tel: 0232 245277

The Royal Bank of Scotland plc
P.O. Box 183
42 St Andrew Square
EDINBURGH EH2 2YE
Tel: 031 556 8555

Ulster Bank Ltd
Avenue House
42/44 Rosemary Street
BELFAST BT1 1QE
Tel: 0232 439674

Yorkshire Bank plc
20 Merrion Way
LEEDS LS2 8NZ
Tel: 0532 441244

B. MATCHED BORROWING

Matched borrowing is a method of obtaining funds which matches the provision against the security of a particular asset. There are three major kinds of matched borrowing:

1. *Factoring* – which provides you with the funds against the security of your sales debtors.

2. *Leasing* – which provides you with fixed assets (computers, vehicles and other equipment) which you use but are owned by the lessor.
3. *Hire purchase* – which provides you with funds to purchase fixed assets against the security of those assets. Both leasing and hire purchase involve your making regular monthly (or quarterly) payments.

Factoring

Factoring companies buy trade debts, releasing up to 80 per cent of the cash due from customers more quickly. The balance is paid when those customers actually pay up. They also take over the day-to-day work of invoicing, sending out statements and debtor accounting.

The service costs between 0.5 and 3.5 per cent of turnover depending on the volume of work, the number of debtors and other related matters.

Should I consider factoring?

Pros

- Lending is linked directly to your sales growth
- It speeds up receipts from sales (quite dramatically)
- It means less bookkeeping – your entire sales ledger is kept for you if you want: for some companies this can save the whole of one clerk's wages (or more)
- It means faster debt collection: your customers are less likely to mess the factor around and the factor is more experienced at debt collection than you are
- It offers insurance against bad debts

Cons

- The cost: you have to pay in terms of interest on the amount advanced and the administration charge which, as it is a percentage of sales, directly reduces your profit per unit
- Loss of customer contact
- Dissatisfaction of customers at having to deal with a factor (although customers who suffer from this probably do so because they are bad payers)

For further information and a list of factors contact:

The Association of British Factors
24–28 Bloomsbury Way
London WC1A 2PX
Tel: 01 831 4268

Leasing

This is a method of obtaining the use of vehicles, plant and equipment without paying the full cost at once. Operating leases are taken out where the equipment will be used for less than its full economic life – for example, a car, photocopier or vending machine. The lessor takes the risk of the equipment becoming obsolete and assumes responsibility for repairs, maintenance and insurance. As the lessee is paying for this service, it is more expensive than a finance lease, where the equipment is leased for most of its economic life and you maintain it and insure it yourself.

Leases can normally be extended, often for fairly nominal sums, in the later years.

The obvious attractions of leasing are that no deposit is needed, leaving working capital for more profitable use elsewhere. Also, the cost of leasing is known from the start, making forward planning more simple.

Should I consider leasing?

Pros

- Payment is by instalments
- You have immediate use of the asset
- VAT can be reclaimed on lease instalments
- At the end of the agreement it is usually possible to extend the lease for a further period by paying a secondary instalment
- The leasing company enjoys a tax benefit and this should be reflected in reduced instalments

Cons

- It is still expensive
- You do not get any capital tax allowances

For further information contact:

The Equipment Leasing Association
18 Upper Grosvenor Street
London W1X 9PB
Tel: 01 491 2783

Hire purchase

This differs from leasing in that users have the option at the start to become the owner of the equipment after a series of payments have been made. The

interest is usually fixed and often more expensive than a bank loan. However, manufacturers (notably car makers) often subsidize this interest, so it pays to shop around both for sources of HP finance and manufacturers of equipment.

Should I consider hire purchase?

Pros
- Payment is by instalments, normally over the life of the asset
- You have immediate use of the asset
- It does not normally affect other bank borrowings
- Full tax capital allowances are available
- VAT is reclaimed on the purchase price

Cons
- It is expensive

For further information and a list of leasing and hire-purchase companies, contact:

The Equipment Leasing Association
18 Upper Grosvenor Street
London W1X 9PB
Tel: 01 491 2783

C. EQUITY

Equity is the term used when you give part ownership of your company to someone else. That ownership can be called equity or share capital. What it means is that, in return for a capital sum, the other person or company has a share in the business; owns part of the assets (in the event of liquidation), has a right to part of the profit (distributed by way of dividends) and has a right to vote on certain issues affecting the business. They also share in the limited liabilities that face shareholders in the event of bankruptcy.

Equity investors are looking for capital growth, with acceptable risks over a time frame of at least five years. They are unlikely to be looking for an immediate stream of income from dividends. Contrast this to loans where the lender is looking for immediate payment of interest and ultimate repayment of capital with minimum risk. A lender does not share in the growth of the business.

You might be able to find individuals who wish to invest and share the risk of your business. This is the most likely source of small amounts of equity capital. However, if you want larger amounts you will probably have to go to one of the many venture capital houses. Venture capital is the term used for risk investments which will involve equity participation but might also involve loans. These equity–loan 'packages' are tailored to meet the individual needs of particular companies. They aim to structure a deal that leaves you with sufficient ownership and control of the business while minimizing the risk the venture capitalist faces with the investment.

Private equity investors

If you are looking for equity investment of less than £100,000 you will probably have to find an individual willing to invest, perhaps using the Business Expansion Scheme (see section below), rather than an institution. There is a network of organizations which may help you find private investors interested in your project. Most charge fees for their services and these vary widely. Since most circulate details of investment opportunities to 'clients' they must either be members of a recognized body like the Stock

Exchange or the Financial Intermediaries, Managers and Brokers Regulatory Association (FIMBRA) or be registered under the terms of the Financial Services Act. Two such organizations are described below.

Local Investment Network Company (LINC)

LINC circulates to subscribing investors a regular bulletin of abbreviated information on business projects. If you are seeking finance through LINC you should submit a business plan indicating the amount of finance required (sample plans and counselling services are available). Having once been accepted as a bona fide proposal you will be charged a small fee for as many bulletin entries (around fifty words) as are felt necessary. Also a longer, two-page summary business plan will be prepared to help any inquirers requesting further details.

You can obtain more details from:

LINC
4 Snow Hill
London EC1A 2BS
Tel: 01 236 3000

Venture Capital Report (VCR)

VCR is a monthly publication of investment opportunities circulated to about 900 subscribers. Each issue contains details of ten or so business projects. VCR charges a flat fee for preparing articles and, in addition, a percentage fee on any risk capital raised.

You can obtain more details from:

VCR
Boston Road
Henley-on-Thames
Berkshire RG9 1DY
Tel: 0491 579999

The Business Expansion Scheme (BES)

The BES is intended to make it attractive for UK income tax payers to invest risk capital into new or growing businesses. The investors must not be connected with the business they invest in. They cannot be paid directors or employers of the business, nor can they own more than 30 per cent of the business. They could, however, be unpaid directors or take fees for professional services. The invester obtains tax relief on up to £40,000 invested in any one year. The minimum investment is £500 and the funds must be left in for at least five years. The effect of this scheme is that a top-rate taxpayer could, for example, by putting £6,000 of his own money into a business secure in return a £10,000 share, the balance being effectively paid by the Inland Revenue.

Venture capital

The UK now has the largest and most diverse venture capital market, outside the USA, with over £2 billion currently invested. Some venture capital houses can provide a range of services beyond equity and loan finance, although in general that is their speciality.

3i

By far the largest venture capital organization is 3i (Investors in Industry), which is owned by the clearing banks and the Bank of England. It offers a very wide range of venture capital and will offer debt/equity deals for anything from start-ups to management buy-outs.

Further details may be obtained from:

3i plc
91 Waterloo Road
London SE1 8XP
Tel: 01 928 7822

British Venture Capital Association

Other venture capital houses have preferences in terms of the types of business they will invest in and how much or how little they will invest, for example, so some research will be needed to find the right company.

The British Venture Capital Association can act as a clearing house for people wishing to locate a source of venture capital.

For further information, contact:

British Venture Capital Association
1 Surrey Street
London WC2R 2PS
Tel: 01 836 5702

Members of the Association

The organisations listed below of the British Venture Capital Association may be contacted direct.

Abacus Development Capital Ltd.
Dammas House
Dammas Lane
Swindon SN1 3EJ
Tel: 0793 618130

Aberdeen Fund Managers Ltd.
10 Queen's Terrace
Aberdeen AB9 1QJ
Tel: 0224 631999

Abingworth plc
26 St James's Street
London SW1A 1HA
Tel: 01 839 6745

Advent Limited
25 Buckingham Gate
London SW1E 6LD
Tel: 01 630 9811

Advent Management
Opportunities Ltd
25 Buckingham Gate
London SW1E 6LD
Tel: 01 630 9811

AIIB Venture Capital
Pinners Hall
8/9 Austin Friars
London EC2N 2AE
Tel: 01 920 9155

Alan Patricof Associates Ltd.
24 Upper Brook Street
London W1Y 1PD
Tel: 01 872 0015

Alta Berkeley Associates
9 Savile Row
London W1X 1AF
Tel: 01 735 4884

B & C Ventures Limited
King's House
36–37 King Street
London EC2V 8BE
Tel: 01 726 4070

Baillie Gifford Technology Ltd.
10 Glenfinlas Street
Edinburgh EH3 6YY
Tel: 031 225 2581

Barclays Development Capital Ltd.
Pickfords Wharf
Clink Street
London SE1 9DG
Tel: 01 407 2389

Barclays Venture Capital Unit
Clerkenwell House
67 Clerkenwell Road
London EC1R 5BH
Tel: 01 242 4900

Baring Brothers Hambrecht & Quist Ltd.
140 Park Lane
London W1Y 3AA
Tel: 01 408 0555

Baring Capital Investors Ltd.
140 Park Lane
London W1Y 3AA
Tel: 01 408 1282

Barnes Thomson Management Ltd.
65 New Cavendish Street
London W1M 7RD
Tel: 01 487 3870

Baronsmead plc
Clerkenwell House
67 Clerkenwell Road
London EC1R 5BH
Tel: 01 242 4900

Birmingham Technology (Venture Capital)
Aston Science Park
Love Lane
Aston Triangle
Birmingham B7 4BJ
Tel: 021 359 0981

British Linen Fund Manager Ltd
32 Melville Street
Edinburgh EH3 7HA
Tel: 031 243 8464

British Technology Group
101 Newington Causeway
London SE1 6BU
Tel: 01 403 6666

Brown Shipley Development Capital Ltd.
Founders Court
Lothbury
London EC2R 7HE
Tel: 01 606 9833

Cambridge Capital Management Ltd.
13 Station Road
Cambridge CB1 2JB
Tel: 0223 312856

Candover Investments plc
Cedric House
8/9 East Harding Street
London EC4A 3ES
Tel: 01 583 5090

Capital Partners International Ltd.
Kingsmead House
250 Kings Road
London SW3 5UE
Tel: 01 351 4899
01 352 3159

Capital Ventures Limited
Rutherford Way
Cheltenham
Glos GL51 9TR
Tel: 0242 584380

Castleforth Fund Managers Ltd.
10 Charterhouse Square
London EC1M 6EH
Tel: 01 490 4113

Causeway Capital Ltd.
21 Cavendish Place
London W1M 9DL
Tel: 01 631 3073

Centreway Development Capital Ltd.
1 Victoria Square
Birmingham B1 1BD
Tel: 021 643 3941

Charterhouse Development Capital Ltd.
7 Ludgate Broadway
London EC4V 6DX
Tel: 01 248 4000

Charterhouse Venture Fund
10 Hertford Street
London W1Y 7DX
Tel: 01 409 3232

Chartfield & Co Ltd.
24/26 Baltic Street
London EC1Y OTB
Tel: 01 608 1451

CIN Venture Managers Ltd.
PO Box 10
London SW1X 7AD
Tel: 01 254 6911

Citicorp Venture Capital Ltd.
PO Box 199
Cotton's Centre
Hay's Lane
London SE1 2QT
Tel: 01 234 5678

Close Investment Management Ltd.
36 Great St Helen's
London EC3A 6AP
Tel: 01 283 2241

Clydesdale Bank Equity Ltd.
30 St Vincent Place
Glasgow G1 2HL
Tel: 041 248 7070

Consolidated Credits
Investment Capital
West World
West Gate
London W5 1DT
Tel: 01 991 2551

County Natwest Ventures Ltd.
Drapers Gardens
12 Throgmorton Avenue
London EC2P 2ES
Tel: 01 382 1000

Creditanstalt Development Capital
29 Gresham Street
London EC2V 7AH
Tel: 01 822 2600

Dartington & Co Securities Ltd.
Bush House
70 Prince Street
Bristol BS1 4QD
Tel: 0272 213206

DCC Ventures Ltd.
103 Mount Street
London W1Y 5HE
Tel: 01 491 0767

Development Capital Group Ltd.
44 Baker Street
London W1M 1DH
Tel: 01 935 2731

E.M. Warburg Pincus & Co
Int. Ltd.
20 St James's Street
London SW1A 1ES
Tel: 01 321 0129

Eagle Star Investment
Managers Ltd.
60 St Mary Axe
London EC3A 8JQ
Tel: 01 929 1111

ECI Ventures
Brettenham House
Lancaster Place
London WC2E 7EN
Tel: 01 606 1000

Electra Innvotec Ltd.
65 Kingsway
London WC2B 6QT
Tel: 01 831 9901

Electra Kingsway Ltd.
65 Kingsway
London WC2B 6QT
Tel: 01 831 6464

Eurocontinental (Advisers) Ltd.
4–6 Throgmorton Street
London EC2N 2AP
Tel: 01 638 6111

Fleming Ventures Ltd.
World Trade Centre
International House
1 St Katherine's Way
London E1 9UN
Tel: 01 480 6211

Foreign & Colonial Ventures Ltd.
6 Laurence Pountney Hill
London EC4R 0BA
Tel: 01 782 9822

Gartmore Investment Ltd.
Gartmore House
16–18 Monument Street
London EC3R 6AJ
Tel: 01 623 1212

Globe Management Ltd.
Globe House
4 Temple Place
London WC2R 3HP
Tel: 01 836 7766

Granville & Co Ltd.
Mint House
77 Mansell Street
London E1 8AF
Tel: 01 488 1212

Greater London Enterprise
63–67 Newington Causeway
London SE1 6BD
Tel: 01 403 0300

Greater Manchester Economic
Dev Ltd.
Bernard House
Piccadilly Gardens
Manchester M1 4DD
Tel: 061 236 4412

Gresham Trust plc
Barrington House
Gresham Street
London EC2V 7HE
Tel: 01 606 6474

Grosvenor Venture Managers Ltd.
Commerce House
2–6 Bath Road
Slough
Berkshire SL1 3RZ
Tel: 0753 32623

Guinness Mahon Development Capital Ltd.
32 St Mary at Hill
London EC3P 3AJ
Tel: 01 623 9333

(GPI) Gyllenhammar & Partners Int. Ltd.
Little Tutton House
3 Dean Trench Street
London SW1P 3HB
Tel: 01 222 8151

Hambro European Ventures Ltd.
41 Tower Hill
London EC3N 4HA
Tel: 01 480 5000

Hambros Advanced Technology Trust plc
20/21 Tooks Court
Cursitor Street
London EC4A 1LB
Tel: 01 242 9900

Hill Samuel Development Capital
100 Wood Street
London EC2P 2AJ
Tel: 01 628 8011

Hodgson Martin Ltd.
36 George Street
Edinburgh EH2 2LE
Tel: 031 226 7647

3i plc
91 Waterloo Road
London SE1 8XP
Tel: 01 928 7822

IC Investment Management Ltd.
1 Adam Street
London WC2N 6AW
Tel: 01 930 1262

Industrial Development Board N. Ireland
IDB House
64 Chichester Street
Belfast BT1 4JX
Tel: 0232 233233

Industrial Technology Securities Ltd.
Omega House
6 Buckingham Place
Bellfield Road
High Wycombe HP13 5HW
Tel: 0494 459923

Ivory & Sime Development Capital
One Charlotte Square
Edinburgh EH2 4DZ
Tel: 031 225 1357

JMI Advisory Services Ltd.
85–87 Jermyn Street
London SW1Y 6JD
Tel: 01 930 7107

Johnston Development Capital Ltd.
Johnston House
Hatchlands Road
Redhill
Surrey RH1 1BG
Tel: 0737 242466

Kent Investments Ltd.
Brenchley House
Week Street
Maidstone
Kent ME14 1RF
Tel: 0622 679976

Kleinwort Benson Development Capital Ltd.
20 Fenchurch Street
London EC3P 3DB
Tel: 01 623 8000

Korda & Company Ltd.
5th Floor
18–20 Farringdon Lane
London EC1R 3AU
Tel: 01 253 5882

Lancashire Enterprises Ltd.
Enterprise House
17 Ribblesdale Place
Winckley Square
Preston PR1 3NA
Tel: 0772 203020

Larpent Newton & Co Ltd.
4th Floor
24/26 Baltic Street
London EC1Y 0TB
Tel: 01 251 9111

Legal & General Ventures Ltd.
Bucklersbury House
3 Queen Victoria Street
London EC4N 8EL
Tel: 01 489 1888

LICA Development Capital Ltd.
102 Jermyn Street
London SW1Y 6EE
Tel: 01 839 7707

Lloyds Development Capital Ltd.
40–66 Queen Victoria Street
London EC4P 4EL
Tel: 01 248 4275
01 236 4940

London Wall Investments
25 Copthall Avenue
London EC2R 7DR
Tel: 01 538 5362

March Investment Fund Ltd.
36–39 Waterfront Quay
Salford Quays
Manchester M5 2XW
Tel: 061 872 3676

Mercury Asset Management
33 King William Street
London EC4R 9AS
Tel: 01 280 2800

Merseyside Enterprise Board Ltd.
Third Floor
Royal Liver Building
Water Street
Liverpool L3 1HT
Tel: 051 236 0221

Midland Montagu Ventures Ltd.
10 Lower Thames Street
London EC3R 6AE
Tel: 01 260 9911

MIM Development Capital Ltd.
11 Devonshire Square
London EC2M 4YR
Tel: 01 626 3434

MTI Managers Ltd.
70 St Albans Road
Watford
Herts WD1 1RP
Tel: 0923 50244

Murray Johnstone Ltd.
7 West Nile Street
Glasgow G1 2PX
Tel: 041 226 3131

Mynshul Ventures Ltd.
Cheshire House
18–20 Booth Street
Manchester M2 4AN
Tel: 061 236 1334

N.M. Rothschild Asset
Management Ltd.
Five Arrows House
St Swithin's Lane
London EC4N 8NR
Tel: 01 280 5000

National Westminster Growth
Options Ltd.
King's Cross House
200 Pentonville Road
London N1 9LH
Tel: 01 239 8563

Newmarket Venture Capital plc
14–20 Chiswell Street
London EC1Y 4TY
Tel: 01 638 2521

North of England Ventures Ltd.
Cheshire House
18–20 Booth Street
Manchester M2 4AN
Tel: 061 236 6600

Northern Venture Managers Ltd.
Centro House
3 Cloth Market
Newcastle upon Tyne NE1 1EE
Tel: 091 232 7068

Norwich Union Venture Capital Ltd.
PO Box No 53
Surrey Street
Norwich NR1 3TE
Tel: 0603 683803

Oakland Investment
Management Ltd.
Ramsbury House
High Street
Hungerford
Berkshire RG17 0LY
Tel: 0488 83555

Octagon Investment
Management Ltd.
Cambridge Science Park
Milton Road
Cambridge CB4 4WE
Tel: 0223 863033

Oxford Seedcord Capital Ltd.
213 Woodstock Road
Oxford OX2 7AD
Tel: 0865 53535

Phildrew Ventures
Triton Court
14 Finsbury Square
London EC2A 1PD
Tel: 01 628 6366

Pine Street Investments Ltd.
Bowater House West
68 Knightsbridge
London SW1X 7LT
Tel: 01 225 3911

Piper Investment Management Ltd.
Eardley House
182–184 Campden Hill Road
London W8 7AS
Tel: 01 727 3866

Prelude Technology
Investments Ltd.
280 Science Park
Milton Road
Cambridge CB4 4WE
Tel: 0223 423132

Prudential Venture Managers Ltd.
Audrey House
Ely Place
London EC1N 6SN
Tel: 01 831 7747

Quayle Munro Ltd.
42 Charlotte Square
Edinburgh EH2 4HQ
Tel: 031 226 4421

Rothschild Ventures Ltd.
New Court
St Swithin's Lane
London EC4P 4DU
Tel: 01 280 5000

Schroder Ventures
20 Southampton Street
London WC2E 7QG
Tel: 01 379 5010

Scimitar Development Capital Ltd.
Osprey House
78 Wigmore Street
London W1H 9DQ
Tel: 01 487 5914

Scottish Development Agency
120 Bothwell Street
Glasgow G2 7JP
Tel: 041 248 2700

Security Pacific Hoare Govett
Equity Ventures Ltd.
4 Broadgate
London EC2M 7LE
Tel: 01 374 1798

Security Pacific Venture Capital
130 Jermyn Street
London SW1Y 4UJ
Tel: 01 925 2395

Seed Capital Ltd.
Boston Road
Henley on Thames
Oxon RG9 1DY
Tel: 0491 579999

Sumit Equity Ventures Ltd.
Edmund House
12 Newhall Street
Birmingham B3 3ER
Tel: 021 200 2244

Sun Life Investment
Management Services Ltd.
107 Cheapside
London EC2V 6DU
Tel: 01 606 7788

Technet Investment Ltd.
63–67 Newington Causeway
London SE1 6BD
Tel: 01 403 0300

The St James's Venture Capital Fund Ltd.
15 St James's Place
London SW1A 1NW
Tel: 01 431 4381

Thompson Clive & Partners Ltd.
24 Old Bond Street
London W1X 3DA
Tel: 01 491 4809

Transatlantic Capital Ltd.
65 Holborn Viaduct
London EC1A 2EU
Tel: 01 489 0021

Ulster Development Capital Ltd.
1 Arthur Street
Belfast BT1 4GA
Tel: 0232 246765

Venture Founders Ltd.
West Court Street
Salamander Quay
Harefield
Uxbridge
Middlesex UP9 6NZ
Tel: 0895 824015

Venture Link Investors Ltd.
Tectonic Place
Holyport Road
Maidenhead
Berkshire SL6 2YG
Tel: 0628 771050

Welsh Development Agency
Pearl House
Greyfriars Road
Cardiff CF1 3XX
Tel: 0222 222666

Welsh Development Capital (Management Ltd.)
Greyfriars Road
Cardiff CF1 3XX
Tel: 0222 378531

West Midlands Enterprise Board Ltd.
31–34 Waterloo Street
Birmingham B2 5TJ
Tel: 021 236 8855

Yorkshire Enterprise Ltd.
Elizabeth House
Queen Street
Leeds LS1 2TW
Tel: 0532 420505

Venture Capital Register

Accountants Peat Marwick McLintock, in conjunction with the journal *Venture Economics*, also maintain a comprehensive database of venture capitalists. This allows them to extract on a selective basis details of various capital sources as potential investment candidates.

> *For further details contact:*
> Peat Marwick McLintock
> 1 Puddle Dock
> Blackfriars
> London EC4V 3PD
> Tel: 01 236 8000

Corporate venturing

You might be able to obtain risk capital from a larger company looking for investments in small ones. The Corporate Venturing Register maintained by the National Economic Development Office (NEDO) contains details of smaller companies seeking large company partners. There is a small fee for registration. All entries are anonymous.

> *For further details contact:*
> NEDO
> Millbank Tower
> Millbank
> London SW1P 4QX
> Tel: 01 217 4000

D. GOVERNMENT AND EC FINANCING SCHEMES

The only UK-wide government scheme is the Loan Guarantee Scheme, which guarantees risky loans to smaller businesses rather than subsidizes them. However, EC loans tend to be at subsidized rates, so they are always worth inquiring about. Also, a number of local authorities offer loans at subsidized rates or with extended periods (called 'soft loans'). It is always worth a phone call to your local council to check whether it has any on offer. Similarly, you should also read Chapter 3 to see whether any of the regional assistance or special schemes for England, Scotland, Wales or Northern Ireland might apply to you.

Government Loan Guarantee Scheme

Small businesses in the UK may be eligible for a loan guarantee under a scheme introduced in 1981.

How the scheme works

1. Guaranteed loans may be for amounts up to £100,000 payable over periods of two to seven years by monthly or quarterly instalments. Capital repayments can be deferred for up to two years. The guarantees are not applicable to overdrafts.
2. The government guarantees 70 per cent of all approved loans, for which a premium of 2.5 per cent is charged, the effect of which is to add 1.75 per cent (i.e. 70 per cent of 2.5 per cent) to the interest charged by the banks.
3. No personal assets or personal guarantees will be taken as security to cover any part of a guaranteed loan. Any personal assets, including the applicant's home, must be already fully committed to secure conventional term loans or overdrafts before a loan guarantee will be considered. All available business assets will be required as security although the absence of these will not exclude consideration under this scheme.
4. Proposals must be in respect of new or additional borrowing requirements for both capital spending and working capital where funds are not available from conventional sources.

Eligible applicants

Applications may be made from sole traders, partnerships, co-operatives and limited companies either already trading or starting up in business. Most goods and services are covered by this scheme but the following are still at present excluded:

(a) agriculture and horticulture;
(b) authors, music composers, and certain own-account artists;
(c) banking and finance;
(d) betting and gambling;
(e) commission agents;
(f) education (other than vocational training, management and business training, driving and flying schools);
(g) forestry (except tree harvesting and sawmilling);
(h) house and estate agents;
(i) insurance services;
(j) libraries, museums, art galleries;
(k) medical – health services;

(l) nightclubs and licensed clubs;
(m) owning and dealing in real estate;
(n) postal services;
(o) professional sport players, sporting organizations (but sports facilities and sports instruction are eligible);
(p) public administration, national defence and compulsory social security;
(q) railways;
(r) telecommunications;
(s) tied public houses and bars;
(t) travel agents (but tour operators are eligible);
(u) veterinary services.

Other matters

The institutions participating in the scheme include all the clearing banks together with many other banks and financial institutions including Investors in Industry (3i). Initial applications under the scheme should be addressed first to your bankers.

With effect from 6 January 1988 simplified administrative procedures were introduced for loans up to £15,000, allowing the major banks to approve loan applications themselves without first referring them to the Department of Employment, thereby speeding up the decision-making process.

Further clarification can be obtained from:

Department of Employment
Caxton House
Tothill Street
London SW1H 9NF
Tel: 01 273 3000

The clearing banks listed in Section A of this chapter will also provide information.

European Coal and Steel Community (ECSC)

ECSC loans are available under its Global Loan Scheme in those areas of the UK listed in Table 5.2, with a view to providing new job opportunities in the coal and steel areas.

Table 5.2 Eligible areas for ECSC Global Loan Schemes

County	Eligible areas	County	Eligible areas
Northumberland	county	Leicestershire	Coalville
Tyne and Wear	county	Nottinghamshire	county
Durham	county	Cheshire	Wrexham
Cleveland	county	Clwyd	Shotton
Cumbria	Workington	Dyfed	Llanlli
Humberside	Scunthorpe	Gwent	county
South Yorkshire	county	South Glamorgan	county
West Yorkshire	Leeds	West Glamorgan	county
	Wakefield	Mid Glamorgan	county
	Castleford	Strathclyde	local authority region
Northamptonshire	Corby		
West Midlands	county	Fife	local authority region
Staffordshire	county		
		Lothian	local authority region

The Scheme, which provides a minimum loan of £15,001, works on the basis that a bank or financial institution, acting as an intermediary, borrows a large tranche of money from ECSC and on-lends smaller 'sub-loans'. These sub-loans may be up to a maximum of 50 per cent of the project's fixed asset and research and development expenditure. The loans are repayable over eight years, with a mandatory capital repayment holiday of four years, and attract a fixed rate of interest. An interest rebate is possible for the first five years of the loan, given acceptable job creation targets, and applicants should inquire as to the current method of calculation for these.

The intermediaries carry out the financial appraisal of the project and need to be satisfied that the proposition is a viable one before seeking approval from ECSC and the DTI.

Applicants must satisfy the following conditions:

(a) be located, or locating in a coal or steel closure area;
(b) be undertaking a new project, which has not yet been started or is under way, involving capital expenditure which is expected to create employment and to be completed within three years.

For further information contact your bank or local regional office of the Department of Trade and Industry (see Chapter 3, Section B).

European Investment Bank (EIB)

EIB is an independent, non profit-making public institution of the Community. It is not funded out of the Community budget, its financial structure being based on capital subscribed by member states, and its operating resources being obtained mainly by borrowing on capital markets. With these resources it provides medium- and long-term loans and guarantees to firms, public authorities and financial institutions to help finance the capital costs of projects which promote:

(a) Regional economic development in the designated national Assisted Areas; or
(b) European integration (e.g. helping to improve communications between member countries or promoting industrial co-operation between firms from different countries); or
(c) European competitiveness (e.g. developing innovative sectors and the use of advanced technology; protecting the environment and/or reducing pollution);
(d) European energy policy (e.g. reducing dependence on oil imports and developing indigenous resources).

EIB will finance up to 50 per cent of the cost of fixed assets needed for the project, with the balance and any working capital provided from other sources. There is no upper limit but generally loans will not be less than £1.0 million. The length of the loan can be between five and twelve years for industrial projects and up to twenty years for infrastructure. Rates of interest are fixed at the time the contract is signed and repayment is normally by equal half-yearly payments of capital and interest. Depending on the project completion date, repayment of principal can be deferred for up to three years. Security is usually a guarantee from the government, a bank or a parent company; exceptionally a loan may be secured on a company's assets.

For further information contact:

Liaison Officer for the UK
European Investment Bank
68 Pall Mall
London SW1Y 5ES
Tel: 01 839 3351

E. OTHER SOURCES OF FINANCE

British Technology Group (BTG)

British Technology Group is a self-financing public organization that licenses new scientific and engineering products to industry and provides finance for the developing of new technology.

Technology transfer

BTG's objective is to promote the development and commercial use of new technology arising from research at UK public sector sources, such as universities, polytechnics, research councils and government research establishments. BTG takes responsibility for protecting the inventions concerned, seeks licences and negotiates licence agreements with industrial companies. Its net revenue is shared with the source on an agreed basis.

Many inventions require further development before being licensed to industry. BTG provides finance for development, usually to the organization at which the initial research was carried out.

Finance for innovation

As part of its technology transfer role BTG can also offer finance to companies that want to develop new products and processes based on their own technology. Through its industrial project finance scheme, BTG can provide up to 50 per cent of the funds required for the development and launching of a new product, and will expect to recover its investment by means of a percentage levy on sales of the resulting product or process.

The subsidiaries of foreign-owned companies are eligible for BTG finance provided that the resulting business will be located in the UK.

Start-up companies

In cases where a particular technology requires a new company to be set up, BTG can perform a catalytic role in promoting the creation of start-up companies.

Further information may be obtained from:

Head of Marketing
British Technology Group
101 Newington Causeway
London SE1 6BU
Tel: 01 403 6666

Industrial Common Ownership Finance Limited (ICOF)

ICOF offers finance to new and expanding worker co-operatives through a revolving loan fund. There is no upper limit to an ICOF loan, but most average £7,500. Capital repayments are normally spread over a five-year period, often commencing on a monthly basis after a six-month holiday. ICOF also works closely with local authorities and operates special loan funds for specific areas, e.g. West Midlands £500,000, West Glamorgan £100,000.

Further information may be obtained from:

ICOF
12–14 Gold Street
Northampton NN1 1RS
Tel: 0604 37563

6 Exporting and Importing

At some stage in its expansion a business will consider exporting or setting up overseas. This may be because, having saturated its niche in the UK market, it is the only way to expand, or because the opportunities overseas are too lucrative to ignore. Exporting normally comes first for a product-based business because it is a less expensive and less risky way of testing an overseas market. However, service businesses generally need to set up abroad to exploit the potential.

With the freeing of trade restrictions within the EC, in advance of 1992, it seems likely that trade with Europe will increase. Not only will there be greater opportunities to export and set up in the other EC countries, there will also be greater opportunities to import attractive products into the UK

market. Indeed, it is expected that many smaller firms will form joint ventures with small firms in other EC countires so that product ranges can be complemented and markets expanded. This strategy has the added advantage of relying upon the local market knowledge of each small firm to market the products of the other.

Market information is the key to successful exporting or importing. Consequently most smaller firms work through agents even when they have researched their market thoroughly. The extensive documentation, exposure to foreign exchange fluctuation risks and problems of debt collection can also prove very daunting to the smaller firm. However, the Export Credits Guarantee Department and your own bank can reduce these problems, for a fee.

A. EXPORTING

Exporting is normally the first step a small firms takes in moving overseas. The Department of Trade and Industry is the major source of help, advice and grant aid to exporters. It draws on the combined resources of its market branches at home and nearly 200 British embassies and consulates around the world. It can supply information on everything from tariffs and regulations to local marketing methods and the economic and commercial climate.

Should I export?

Pros	Cons
• Increases demand for your product	• You will not know the market as well as the UK
• Allows you to charge differential prices	• You may be exposed to fluctuations in foreign currencies
• You can diversify out of the risk of operating in only one economy	• You may have problems collecting debts
• You might benefit from economies of scale	• You will have to deal with more documentation

The Department of Trade and Industry (DTI)

The DTI is at:
1 Victoria Street
London SW1H 0ET
Tel: 01 215 7877

It also operates out of ten regional offices which were part of the old British Overseas Trade Board's Area Advisory Groups. These offices are listed below:

DTI regional offices

England

North East
Stanegate House
2 Groat Market
Newcastle upon Tyne NE1 1YN
Tel: 091 232 4722

North West
Sunley Tower
Piccadilly Plaza
Manchester M1 4BA
Tel: 061 236 2171

Yorkshire and Humberside
Priestley House
3–5 Park Row
Leeds LS1 5LF
Tel: 0532 443171

East Midlands
Severns House
20 Middle Pavement
Nottingham NG1 7DW
Tel: 0602 506181

West Midlands
Ladywood House
Stephenson Street
Birmingham B2 4DT
Tel: 021 632 4111

South East
Bridge Place
Eccleston Square
London SW1V 1PT
Tel: 01 215 7877

South West
5th Floor
The Pithay
Bristol BS1 2PB
Tel: 0272 272666

Scotland

Scottish Export Office
Industry Department for Scotland
Alhambra House
45 Waterloo Street
Glasgow G2 6AT
Tel: 041 248 2855

Wales

Welsh Office
Industry Department
New Crown Building
Cathays Park
Cardiff CF1 3NQ
Tel: 0222 825396

Northern Ireland

Industrial Development Board for Northern Ireland
IDB House
64 Chichester Street
Belfast BT1 4JX
Tel: 0232 233233

The Marketing Initiative

The DTI's Marketing Initiative provides independent, professional advice on a company's export potential; how it should plan for exporting and how it should go about selecting the right markets.

The scheme is run for the DTI by the Institute of Marketing and offers from five to fifteen days of subsidized consultancy from an export specialist. The DTI will pay half the costs – two-thirds if the company is in an Assisted or Urban Programme Area. The scheme would be particularly valuable for a company thinking of exporting for the first time or of expanding existing exporting activity. It is available to companies employing fewer than 500 people.

The company will first receive a free business review by an Enterprise Counsellor to identify the scope of a subsidized consultancy. Further information can be obtained from your local DTI regional office.

Market Branches

There are nine Market Branches located at the DTI headquarters. They form the focus for all information about trading in individual countries and are in touch with the commercial staff in the 200 or so UK embassies, high commissions and consulates abroad.

Market Branches' information covers tariffs and regulations, business customs and the economic climate. Often they can advise on market prospects, the competition, the prospects for a product and the best way of tackling the market.

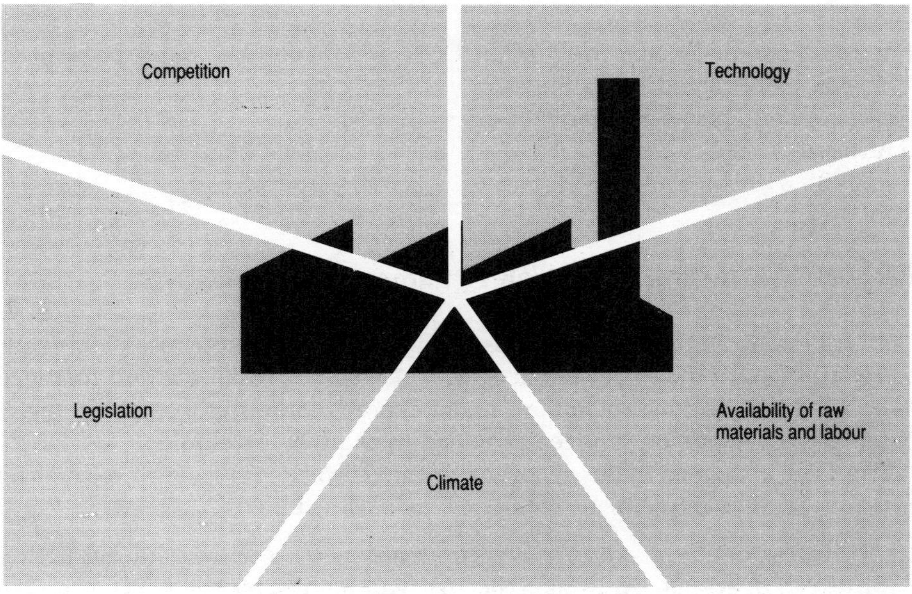

Market branch inquiry numbers

These are as follows:

North America
Industrial Goods
Tel: 01 215 4604/4608

Southern Africa
Tel: 01 215 5011

Consumer Goods
Tel: 01 215 4593/4595

Medical, Scientific and Commodities
Tel: 01 215 5185/4563

Western Europe
Tel: 01 215 5336

Eastern Europe
Tel: 01 215 5258

Middle East
Tel: 01 215 4388

Latin America
Tel: 01 215 5056

Australia/New Zealand
Tel: 01 215 5319/5321/4760/4759

Caribbean
Tel: 01 215 5297

West Africa
Tel: 01 215 4967

South Africa
Tel: 01 215 5011

Japan
Industrial Goods
Tel: 01 215 4803/4801

Consumer Goods
Tel: 01 215 4801/4802

South East Asia
Tel: 01 215 4742

South Asia
(India, Sri Lanka, Pakistan, Bangladesh, Nepal)
Tel: 01 215 4825

China
Tel: 01 215 5252/4827

Hong Kong
Tel: 01 215 4729

For tariff inquiries, the product's CCCN or HS number must be quoted. This can be obtained by calling:
Customs and Excise Statistical Office
Southend-on-Sea
Tel: 0702 348944.

Export Marketing Research Scheme

This DTI scheme offers free professional advice to UK business and trade associations on how to set about export marketing research, and financial support if it is decided to embark on an export marketing research project. Exporters of goods or services provided in the UK are eligible.

The DTI is able to make generous grants towards the cost of marketing research studies in overseas countries, as outlined below.

1. If professional consultants are commissioned to undertake marketing research overseas, up to half the cost will be met by the DTI.
2. If a company's own staff have the ability and experience to carry out marketing research to a satisfactory professional standard, the DTI will support 'in-house' marketing research studies outside the European Community. The DTI will pay half of essential travel costs and interpreters' fees, plus a daily allowance for time spent overseas by a researcher.

3. The DTI will pay up to a third of the cost of purchasing published marketing research (but not for directories or market overviews or for updating subscriptions).

Advice on preparing a proposal for submission to the Export Marketing Research Section is available on request.

Trade associations commissioning research or carrying out 'in house' overseas marketing research on behalf of their members will receive up to 75 per cent of the cost from the DTI.

For individual companies two projects can be supported per year, plus the purchase of two published market research studies, subject to a maximum grant of £20,000 per project and an aggregate limit of £40,000 of grant per year. These restrictions do not apply to trade associations.

Further information may be obtained from:

Export Marketing Research Section
The Association of British Chambers of Commerce
4 Westwood House
Westwood Business Park
Coventry CV4 8HS
Tel: 0203 694484

Trade fairs overseas

These are three schemes designed to encourage businesses to participate in overseas trade fairs with a view to increasing exports of UK goods and services. In each case the DTI provides space (normally 15 square metres) and a shell stand, together with some display facilities, at attractive rates to firms taking part in group displays of UK products at overseas trade fairs. Additionally, for events taking place outside Western Europe, exhibitors in the group may be eligible for travel grants.

The Joint Venture Scheme

This involves a number of businesses in an industry taking part, with DTI support, in a collective presentation of UK goods or services at a specialized trade fair overseas under the sponsorship of an approved trade association, chamber of commerce or other approved non-profit-making body. The minimum number of businesses acceptable in a joint venture is normally around ten. Charges vary according to whether inside or outside space is taken and whether it is a first-time, second-time or subsequent exhibitor; a larger area may sometimes be provided it it can be justified and if sufficient space is available. Special terms are available for British groups exhibiting at trade fairs in Japan.

The British Pavilion Scheme

Provided enough businesses wish to participate, the DTI will organize British pavilions at certain international trade fairs overseas (mainly outside Western Europe) to display UK exhibits. Companies will be charged part of the DTI's estimated direct costs, first-time exhibitors at a particular event, being particularly favoured.

All-British exhibitions

In overseas markets which are considered to be actually or potentially of special importance but where there are no suitable international trade fairs the DTI may organize special all-British exhibitions. The exhibitions may be specialized or of a general industrial nature. There is no common fee and the charge to participants is announced at the same time as the event.

The full programme of support for UK industry at overseas trade fairs is published at quarterly intervals in the *Trade Promotions Guide*, which is a supplement to *British Business*, a weekly magazine from the DTI. In addition, the DTI's Export Intelligence Service includes from time to time information about the organization of pavilions and all-British fairs.

Further information may be obtained from:

Department of Trade and Industry
Fairs and Promotions Branch
Dean Bradley House
52 Horseferry Road
London SW1P 2AG
Tel: 01 276 2414

Overseas seminars

Under this scheme the DTI may support seminars organized outside the UK. To qualify for support, events must bring specific UK products, processes or services which correspond with known needs or interests to the attention of equally specific buyers, users and technological experts.

Only seminars organized and sponsored by a trade association or other non-profit-making body in association with the DTI can be considered for support, and the extent of the prospective commercial benefit for the UK determines whether or not support will be given.

Normally, proposals must be made twelve months before the event and each business taking part in a seminar or symposium under this scheme will be charged at a rate intended to cover 55 per cent of the estimated direct cost of the hire of the auditorium and other equipment, translation fees and lecture interpreters, local publicity and additional local staff costs.

Up to two persons per firm travelling from the UK to read a paper at a seminar held outside Western Europe can obtain travel support at the rate applicable to the DTI Outward Mission Scheme (see next subsection), if the destination is a country included under that scheme.

Sometimes a seminar can benefit from a modest on-the-spot associated exhibition. Terms are as for the seminar scheme with support covering space rental and graphics, etc. Additional travel grants can be claimed for up to two stand representatives provided they are presenting papers.

Outward Mission Scheme

The DTI provides assistance to groups of British exporters travelling as a mission sponsored by an approved trade association, chamber of commerce or other approved non-profit-making body to visit overseas markets, either to explore and assess the prospects for their goods or services, or to reinforce their overseas marketing effort. Participants in missions are not required to be members of the sponsoring body.

The scheme applies to missions covering British products or services which have promise in the market, or to planned promotions which are selected for official support.

Normally the minimum number of members of a mission qualifying for support will be ten and the maximum twenty, and financial assistance will be limited to one representative of any UK business.

Each participant in a mission approved for support under this scheme may claim after the event a contribution towards his or her costs, according to a scale of rates for different countries. Most but not all overseas markets are covered by this scheme;

Inward Mission Scheme

Under this scheme financial assistance is offered to groups of businesses wishing to bring to the UK overseas buyers, journalists, or others who can influence exports. The visitors must undertake a joint programme of visits and this programme must therefore be confirmed to a narrow range of goods or services of common interest to the visitors.

To qualify for assistance an inward mission must be sponsored by a non-profit-making organisation, normally a trade association, but all UK businesses in the industry concerned are eligible for participation whether or not they belong to the sponsoring body.

Assistance will be 50 per cent of the direct economy class return for mission members coming from Western Europe and Algeria, Cyprus, Finland, Gibraltar, Libya, Malta, Morocco, Tunisia and Yugoslavia, 75 per cent of those from elsewhere, plus 50 per cent of other essential costs such as travel in the UK, hotel accommodation, and interpretation and reception fees.

The average number of invitees is ten, although up to twenty will be considered. Invitations are usually limited to one representative of each overseas company. Six to eight months' notice should be given.

Major business projects and the Overseas Projects Fund

The Projects and Export Policy Division (PEP) of the DTI co-ordinates the support given by government for industry in pursuing major projects overseas and for advising on related policy. These projects will normally offer a UK content of more than £20 million, although consultancies with a lower value are also supported. It is also responsible for the administration of the Overseas Projects Fund.

Assistance from the Fund can be given towards the pre-contractual costs of major capital projects overseas which require a package or turnkey approach. The Fund may also contribute to the cost of feasibility studies for major projects.

Assistance from the Fund is given only where its availability is likely to increase the chances of winning a contract and is normally repayable if the contract is won. The amount of assistance is assessed according to the individual circumstances of the project and the applicant will normally be expected to meet the bulk of costs.

Export Representative Service

This service provides help in deciding the right person abroad to act as agent, distributor or importer. Assistance can also be given in finding a manufacture-under-licence partner.

Information about the UK company is sent to the British embassy or other diplomatic post in the country concerned and it will contact suitable potential representatives known to be experienced and reliable. A report will be passed back to the company giving names and addresses of agents specifically interested and qualified to represent the company's interest.

The cost of this service varies depending on the country concerned.

Companies which buy the report and subsequently follow it up with a visit to the market within six months will be eligible for a refund of their travel costs up to 50 per cent of the charge for the report.

The service is available to all companies not represented in a particular area, or whose existing agent has been given notice of termination, or where a new product line not covered by existing arrangements is introduced. The only countries not covered are those of the Communist bloc, and some countries in the middle East and North Africa.

Contact your regional DTI office (listed earlier in this section) for further details.

Other sources of advice and help

Central Office of Information (COI)

The COI is the government's main publicity outlet and provides an export publicity operation which helps UK business to boost its sales throughout the world.

The COI comprises professional journalists, photographers, script-writers, film-makers and designers who specialize in industrial, trade, technical and commercial news stories. Businesses should therefore inform the COI of any newsworthy items which may be publicized with a view to boosting their names in overseas markets. The COI works closely with the DTI.

Further information may be obtained from:

Central Office of Information
Hercules Road
London SE1 7DU
Tel: 01 928 2345

Export Credit Guarantee Department (ECGD)

The ECGD is the UK's main export credit insurer, providing a wide range of credit insurance services. It insures exporters against the risk of not being paid, whether through the default of the buyer or through other causes, such as restrictions on the transfer of currency, cancellation of valid import licenses, etc. It furnishes guarantees of repayment to banks; on this security the exporters' banks provide finance for exports at sometimes favourable interest rates. This facility is available for exports of capital goods sold on credit terms of two years or more. ECGD cover may provide access to finance for exports on shorter terms of credit.

The ECGD also insures new investment overseas against the risks of war, expropriation and the restriction of remittances. It supports the issue of performance bonds, and, for members of a UK consortium, provides protection from loss caused by the insolvency or withdrawal of a member of the consortium.

Further information, including the ECGD handbook ECGD Services, may be obtained from:

ECGD
PO Box 272
Export House
50 Ludgate Hill
London EC4M 7AY
Tel: 01 382 7000

Simplification of International Trade Procedures Board (SITPRO)

SITPRO was established in 1970 to guide, stimulate and assist the rationalization of international trade procedures and documentation. It operates on an annual grant from the DTI and income from sales of its materials and services. The Board and working group membership is drawn from a wide range of commercial and official interests including carriers, shippers, freight forwarders, bankers, HM Customs, etc. The Board's concern is that recent improvements in transport and data transmission have not been matched by corresponding improvements in trade procedures and documentation.

The Board negotiates the simplification and reduction of paperwork required in international trade. Similarly, when organizations propose to revise their trade procedures SITPRO seeks to ensure that these changes are effected in a manner least likely to cause complications for those engaged in international trade.

A number of simplified trade procedures have been developed, e.g. a range of customs export procedures to suit different company situations; alternatives to traditional bills of lading; Dangerous Goods Note to establish a standard practice for all such goods exported by sea, road or rail; the Standard Shipping Note and many others.

Further details and a range of booklets and leaflets may be obtained from:

SITPRO
Venture House
29 Glasshouse Street
London W1R 5RG
Tel: 01 287 3525

Institute of Export

The Institute aims to contribute to profitable exporting by providing a forum for the exchange of experience and information between exporters. It also promotes education and training throughout the whole field of exporting. Its regular journal, *Export*, is a good way of getting into the export picture.

The Institute's address is:

Institute of Export
64 Clifton Street
London EC2A 4HB
Tel: 01 247 9812

Exporters' workshops

The Small Firms Group of the London Chamber of Commerce provides information, education and contacts to help small firms to start exporting. Your local chamber may do the same.

Further information from:

Small Firms Group
London Chamber of Commerce
69 Cannon Street
London EC4N 5AB
Tel: 01 248 4444

Export Buying Offices' Association

The Association assists in the exporting of consumer products to the department stores of the world, which are its members.

It can be contacted at:

Export Buying Offices' Association
c/o Portman Ltd
360 Oxford Street
London W1A 4BX
Tel: 01 493 8141

Export houses

There are some 800 export houses operating in the UK, offering almost every service possible to exporters and foreign importers. Some 230 of them belong to the British Exporters Association, and they are actively interested in working with small firms.

Three types of company will find an export house particularly useful: those considering exporting for the first time; those that want to expand outside their existing overseas markets; and those that have to extend credit to their customers to a greater extent than they are willing or able to (this may be to meet competition or currency problems).

Export houses are specialists in financing and servicing exports and are divided into four main types.

Export agents and managers

They sell a manufacturer's goods in selected countries where they have expert knowledge. They work very closely with their clients, and can in effect become the manufacturer's own export department. This can save a small company money and provide a greater level of expertise than could realistically be afforded. Payment for these services is usually by commission, but sometimes a retainer or even a profit-sharing scheme can be used.

Confirming houses

Confirming houses represent foreign buyers in the UK and can confirm, as a principal, an order placed by that buyer with a British supplier. Buying or independent houses buy, pay for and ship goods for their overseas principals. A stores buyer is a particular type of buying house dealing only with departmental stores. Being linked to such houses costs you nothing but can open up many new overseas markets for your products.

Merchants

As the word implies, merchants both buy and sell as a principal. They specialize in certain products and markets. One of the largest sells in 120 different countries. Others operate in a much narrower sphere. Dealing with a merchant is little different from selling in the UK and, even better, there is no credit risk.

Finance houses

They can provide you with non-resource finance and allow your foreign buyer time to pay. This gives the exporter absolute security and makes the deal attractive to an overseas buyer. Normally only the foreign buyer pays a commission for the service.

British Exporters Association

This is the best starting point for contacting an export house. The Association provides a *Directory of British Export Houses*, which tells you all about each house and its particular expertise. Alternatively, full details of prospective exports requirements can be included, at a cost, in the Association's monthly *Export Enquiry* circular. The circular goes to all members and is considered to be a very effective way of communicating quickly in a rapidly changing environment.

The Association can be contacted at:

British Exporters Association
16 Dartmouth Street
Westminster
London SW1H 9BL
Tel: 01 222 5419

Birmingham Chamber of Industry and Commerce

The Chamber keeps an up-to-date list of overseas contracts that are open to tender and other major export opportunities. Public sector contracts in EC countries must be open to tender from any company in any other member state and preference can no longer be given, after 1992, to local firms.

It can be contacted at:

Birmingham Chamber of
Industry and Commerce
75 Harborne Road
Birmingham B15 3DH
Tel: 021 454 6171

Banks and accountants

Many of the clearing banks have, or are developing, international branch networks. These can give you invaluable local advice about overseas trade opportunites, as well as offering financial services to exporters. In the first instance, contact your own bank and ask for details.

Many of the larger firms of accountants produce guides to doing business in specific countries. These include information on local markets, laws and taxation. They are normally provided free as part of their client service. For example, Arthur Andersen & Co. produces a series of tax and trade guides on overseas countries.

The firm is at:

Arthur Andersen & Co.
1 Surrey Street
London WC2R 2PS
Tel: 01 836 1200

Sources of information

Export Market Information Centre

This library is primarily concerned with statistics and directories from overseas countries and import/export data on the UK. As such it is the most important source of international statistics and business information.

It is located at:

Export Market Information Centre
1 Victoria Street
London SW1H 0ET
Tel: 01 215 5444/5
Reading room open
Monday–Friday, 0930–1730

The following directories on overseas countries will give a flavour of the data contained in the Library, or in other major reference libraries.

Principal International Business

Published by Dun & Bradstreet, the directory gives the basic facts about 50,000 businesses in 135 countries. As well as the business name, address and telex and its main activities, it tells you if the company is a subsidiary of a larger corporation; whether it imports or exports; how many employees it has; latest sales volume; and the name of the chief executive. Its cover of companies in each country is not great; nearly 8,000 in the USA; 6,000 in Germany; 5,500 in France; 4,000 in Japan; and 2,000 businesses in the UK. This represents only a small percentage of the businesses in any one country, but they are the principal ones.

Concise Guide to Standard and Poor's Register of Corporations

The Corporation Record, Volume I, has a wealth of information on the financial structure and performance of 38,000 of the most significant American corporations. There is also a list of subsidiary companies cross-referenced to parents. Volume II contains the individual listings of 70,000 people serving as officers of these corporations, together with some personal details on their education and fraternal membership. Volume III contains a series of indexes that complement the first two volumes.

Thomas's Register of American Manufacturers

This consists of sixteen volumes, making it probably the most comprehensive directory on the market. Volumes 1–8 list products alphabetically, giving the manufacturer's name. Volumes 9 and 10 give company names, addresses with zip codes and telephone numbers listed alphabetically, together with branch offices, capital ratings and company officials. An American trade-mark index is given in Volume 10.

Volumes 11–16, called *Thomcat*, contain catalogues of companies, bound alphabetically and cross-referenced in the first ten volumes. In sum, a formidable work, useful either to find an American source of supply or a potential customer for your product. The catalogues provide an insight into the way in which American companies market their waves. (Other similar directories are available for most advanced industrial countries.)

Wall Street's corporate and industry research reports

Prepared by leading analysts and UK brokerage and institutional investment firms, these reports provide in-depth analysis and data on 5,000 companies and 150 industries, prepared by forty research departments.

Concise Guide to International Markets

Now published in four volumes, covering Europe, the Americas, the Far East and Australia, and the Middle East and Africa, the *Concise Guide* is updated every two years, and contains 4,000 facts about 109 world markets. There are 550 pages of up-to-date information on population, literacy, languages, religion, climate, working hours, currency, main towns, income, retail and wholesale structures, advertising agencies, commissions, associations, and advertising controls, advertising expenditure, media of all types and market research facilities, together with over 100 maps.

This guide provides a useful overview to markets, and could be helpful in choosing markets to look at more closely later.

Croner's Reference Book for Exporters

This is a loose-leaf, regularly updated service that keeps exporters up to date on all exporting procedures. It is available on a ten-day free approval offer.

Croner's is available from:

Croner Publications Ltd
Croner House
London Road
Kingston upon Thames
Surrey KT2 6SR
Tel: 01 547 3333

Directory of Export Buyers in the UK

The conventional wisdom of successful exporting recommends that you should travel abroad to contact buyers. However, firms abroad are increasingly establishing buying offices in this country in order, among other reasons, to look for new sources of supply. It is estimated that orders for about 20 per cent of British exports are negotiated and signed in the UK, and mainly by people listed in this directory. The entries are indexed by countries bought from, products bought and foreign firms bought for.

Details from:

Trade Research Publications
6 Beech Hill Court
Berkhamstead
Herts HP4 2PR
Tel: 0442 863951

Export Intelligence Service

Speed is the essence of the Export Intelligence Service, a computer-based yet personalized daily market intelligence service giving information about overseas markets and export opportunities. As many as 10,000 different products or services are separately identified, and coverage is literally worldwide.

In addition to sales leads, the service provides details of calls for tender, agents seeking UK principals, early notification of overseas projects and many other trade opportunities.

It is available on a subscription basis: you may either pay separately for each 'notice' of information, or an annual subscription for everything. (The service published nearly 50,000 notices in 1988.)

Overseas Status Report Service (OSRS)

OSRS provides information about the interests and capabilities of overseas companies, which may help a UK exporter in deciding whether or not to enter into a business relationship with them.

There is a charge for the overseas status reports, and further information may be obtained from the appropriate DTI regional office (listed earlier in this section).

Technical Help to Exporters (THE)

THE is a DTI service operated by the British Standards Institution (BSI). THE exists to help exporters identify and comply with standards, certification and other technical requirements which exist in markets overseas.

THE provides the following services.

1. A technical inquiry service to deal with the day-to-day identification of standards or other technical requirements overseas.
2. A consultancy service to undertake in-depth investigation and offer advice on the application of these technical requirements to the design and manufacture of products and equipment.
3. Special updating services to specific sectors of industry to maintain all relevant standards and other technical documents.
4. Publication sales, including all foreign national standards and other nationally recognized documents, together with THE's own surveys and reports on overseas requirements.
5. A technical translation service providing English translations of a wide range of important overseas standards and regulations,

These services are available to both members and non-members of The BSI. Any company in the UK is eligible for membership of The BSI. A charge is made for services provided but non-members pay a higher rate than members, who also have the use of the library and an invoicing facility.

Further information may be obtained from:

Technical Help to Exporters
British Standards Institution
Linford Wood
Brecklands
Milton Keynes MK14 6LE
Tel: 0908 220022

B. IMPORTING

British Importers Confederation

The Confederation was founded in 1972, and represents some 3,500 importers. It is the only organization protecting the interests of importers whatever the goods concerned.

Membership fees are modest and members include a significant number of one-man importers or smaller firms, as well as such companies as Shell and Unilever.

Because of its close relationship with the UK government and the EC Commissions, the Confederation is usually aware of likely changes in import procedures long before they occur. This knowledge and other information form an important part of the service the Confederation can provide for small businesses.

Further information may be obtained from:

British Importers Confederation
69 Cannon Street
London EC4N 5AB
Tel: 01 248 4444

Sources of information

The directories mentioned below can be found at the Export Market Information Centre (listed in Section A: Exporting) or at other major reference libraries.

Croner's Reference Book for Importers

Croner's accurately spells out the regulations and procedures to import goods of any nature into the UK. It covers import controls, exchange controls, VAT, marketing of goods, customs and excise, and transit and transhipment insurance. The book is in loose-leaf form and the service includes a regular supply of updates. It is available from Croner Publications - address in Section A: Exporting.

Directory of British Importers

This is published by the British Importers Confederation and Trade Research Publications. The *Directory* gives a considerable amount of information about importing firms, and whether you simply want to find out more about your competitors or to find an alternative source of supply, it will give you the answers. The Confederation also produces a handbook on importing.

7 Business and the Law

Most laws affect small family companies, partnerships and sole traders in exactly the same way as they affect larger companies and corporations. Larger firms may have whole departments to interpret the ever-growing mountain of legislation. In smaller firms it is often the owner–manager or directors who shoulder the burden of finding their way through the legislative maze and try to avoid these, often underestimated, consequences of blissful ignorance.

This chapter of the Handbook should draw your attention to some of the legal responsibilities of being in business. Survival may depend on your understanding the many implications of the law and keeping up to date with changes. It does *not* equip you to be your own lawyer although in some clear-cut situations you may be tempted to go it alone to save costs. However, it is often not worthwhile to resort to the law in terms of either money, time or sheer emotional energy. It is one thing to know your rights – another to enforce them. Take advantage of your solicitor's knowledge of the law if it comes to it but for the moment try to find out as much as you can about the legal framework within which you operate.

A. WHAT FORM SHOULD YOUR BUSINESS TAKE?

It is important to decide early on which of four possible legal forms your business should take. The one chosen will depend on a number of factors – for example commercial needs, financial risk, status and the tax position. Your decision is not irrevocable but putting right mistakes can be costly, in both time and money. Your choice of structure provides the legal framework within which you will operate. These forms are summarized below.

Sole trader?

This is the simplest way to start up in business. As a sole trader you can trade on your own account without taking any particular legal steps. If your own name is being used for the business, it doesn't need registration. If you decide to trade under a different name you must remember to include your own on the headed paper. Unless the business is past the VAT threshold there are no rules about the records to be kept although it would be prudent to keep good books and take professional advice at the outset. You will need to tell your local tax inspector you are becoming self-employed (Form 41G) and your local DHSS office.

A sole trader is personally liable for the debts of his or her business, so in the event of failure you could lose your personal possessions as well as the business assets.

Pros	Cons
• Minimum paperwork • Start trading immediately • No set-up costs • No audit fees • No public disclosure of trading information • Pay Schedule D tax • Profit or loss in one trade can be offset against another • Past PAYE can be clawed back to help with trading losses	• Unlimited personal liability for trading debts • No access to equity capital • When you die, so does the business

Partnership?

There are very few restrictions to setting up in business with another person (or persons) in partnership. Many partnerships are entered into without legal formalities and sometimes without the parties themselves being aware that they have entered into a partnership.

All that is needed is for two or more people to agree to carry on a business together intending to share the profits. The law will then recognize the existence of a partnership.

Most of the points raised when considering sole tradership apply to partnerships. All the partners are personally liable for the debts of the partnership, even if those debts were incurred by one partner's mismanagement or dishonesty without the other partner's knowledge.

A partnership contract

Before entering into a partnership it is vital to take legal advice in drawing up a partnership contract. The contract should cover the following points:

Profit sharing, responsibilities and duration

This should specify how profits and losses are to be shared, and who is to carry out which tasks. It should also set limits on partners' monthly drawings, and on how long the partnership itself is to last (either a specific period of years or indefinitely, with a cancellation period of, say, three months).

Voting rights and policy decisions

Unless otherwise stated, all the partners have equal voting rights. It is advisable to define 'policy' or 'voting decision', and how such decisions are to be made. You must also decide how to expel a partner or admit a new one.

Time off

Every partner is entitled to his share of the profits even when ill or on holiday. You will need some guidelines on the length and frequency of holidays, and on what to do if someone is absent for a long period for any other reason.

Withdrawing capital

You have to decide how each partner's share of the capital of the business will be valued in the event of a partner leaving or the partnership being dissolved.

Accountancy procedure

You do not have either to file accounts or to have accounts audited. However, it may be prudent to agree a satisfactory standard of accounting and employ a firm of accountants to carry out that work. Sleeping partners may well insist on it.

Sleeping partners

A partner who has put up capital but does not intend to take an active part in running the business can protect himself against risk by having his partnership registered as a limited partnership.

Pros	Cons
• No audit required, though your partner may insist on one • No public disclosure of trading information	• Unlimited personal liability for your own and your partner's trading debts (except sleeping partners) • Partnership contracts can be complex and costly to prepare • Limited access to equity capital • Death of a partner usually causes partnership to be dissolved

Franchise?

This is a rapidly growing area of small business and is essentially a mutually dependent partnership agreement which can be between sole traders, partnerships or companies. The franchisor licenses a package of rights and imposes a number of controls, usually financial and quality controls, to afford protection. The franchisee pays a fee, royalty and/or dividend to the franchisor and conforms to the set 'style' laid down in the terms of the agreement (which will have been professionally drafted to comply with UK and EC law relating to unfair competition and restraint of trade).

For information on franchising, contact:

British Franchise Association
Thames View
Newtown Road
Henley-on-Thames
Oxfordshire RG9 1HG
Tel: 0491 578049

Limited company?

If your business takes this form you have no choice but to comply with rules laid down in the Companies Act. The main distinction between a limited company and a partnership or sole trader is that it has a legal identity of its own separate from the people who own it. This means that, in the event of liquidation, creditors' claims are restricted to the assets of the company. The shareholders are not liable as individuals for the business debts beyond the nominal value of their shares. This applies even if the shareholders are working directors, unless the company has been trading fraudulently or wrongfully.

The Insolvency Act 1986 among other things brings into effect the notion that limited liability is a privilege rather than a right. Under these new rules incompetent as well as fraudulent directors may incur a measure of personal liability for debts incurred in the face of looming insolvency.

Directors found unfit to manage can also be disqualified from holding office elsewhere.

Other advantages for limited companies include the freedom to raise capital by selling shares and certain tax advantages.

The disadvantages include the legal requirements for the company's accounts to be audited by a chartered or certified accountant, and for certain records of the business trading activities to be filed annually at Companies House.

In practice, the ability to limit liability is severely restricted by the requirements of potential lenders. They often insist on personal guarantees from directors when small, new or troubled companies look for loans or credits. The personal guarantee usually takes the form of a charge on the family house. Since the *Boland* case, in 1980, unless a wife has specifically agreed to take a charge on the house, by signing a deed of postponement, then no lender can take possession in the case of default.

A limited company can be formed by two shareholders, one of whom must be a director. A company secretary must also be appointed, who can be a shareholder, director or an outside person such as an accountant.

The company can be bought 'off the shelf' from a registration agent, then adapted to suit your own purposes. This will involve changing the name, the shareholders and the articles of association.

Alternatively, a solicitor or accountant can form a 'tailor made' company.

Pros

- Shareholders' liabilities restricted to nominal value of shares
- It is possible to raise equity capital
- High status public image
- If income is substantial, corporation tax for a small business is lower than equivalent income tax rate
- The business has a life of its own and continues with or without the founder

Cons

- Directors are on PAYE
- Audit required
- Trading information must be disclosed
- Suppliers, landlords and banks will probably insist on personal guarantees from directors (except for government loan guarantee scheme)
- You cannot start trading until you have a certificate of incorporation

If you are unsure about your position contact:

Companies Registration Office
Companies House
Crown Way
Maindy
Cardiff CF4 3UZ
Tel: 0222 388588

Co-operative?

The fifth form of business is for people whose primary concern is to create a democratic work environment, sharing profits and control. If you want to control or substantially influence your own destiny and make as large a capital gain out of your life's work as possible, a co-operative is not for you.

You need seven founder members to register and the membership of the co-operative is the legal body that controls the business. A member is anyone who shares in the control of the co-op, and must be either a worker or a founder member. At least half the employees should be members. The co-operative must be registered under the Industrial and Provident Societies Acts 1965–75 with the Chief Registrar of Friendly Societies. You could organize the co-operative as a company limited by guarantee, which has the advantage of needing only two people to form it.

For information on co-operatives, contact:

The Co-operative Development Agency
Broadmead House
21 Panton Street
London SW1Y 4DR
Tel: 01 839 2987

Generally, for further advice on choosing the legal form of your business contact a solicitor or accountant.

B. BUSINESS NAMES

The name you choose now for your business should be the name you still have in five or ten years' time. Describing what your business does through the name you choose is a cheap but effective means of communicating your message to potential and existing customers.

Since 26 February 1982, when the provision of the Companies Act 1981 came into effect, there have been new rules affecting the choice of business name.

First, anyone wanting to use a 'controlled' name will have to obtain permission. There are some eighty or ninety controlled names, that include words such as 'international', 'bank', and 'royal'. This is simply to prevent a business implying that it is something it is not.

Second, all businesses that intend to trade under names other than those of their owner(s) must state who does own the business and how the owner can be contacted. So, sole traders or partnerships who use surnames with or without forenames or initials, are not affected if they simply use their full corporate name.

If any name other than the 'true' name is to be used, the name of the owner(s) must be disclosed and an address in the UK given, to which the business documents can be sent. This information must be shown on all business letters, on orders for goods and services, invoices and receipts, and statements and demands for business debts. Also, a copy must be displayed prominently on all business premises. The purpose of the Act is simply to make it easier to 'see' with whom business is being done.

For further information and two useful free publications - notes for guidance on *Disclosure of Business Ownership* and *Control of Business Names* - contact:

The Department of Trade and Industry
Guidance Notes Section
55 City Road
London ECIY 1BB
Tel: 01 253 9393

C. PROTECTING IDEAS

You may feel the process of protecting your original ideas, the life-blood of your business, is time consuming and expensive. There are, however, numerous examples of businesses that have failed because they have neglected this important area.

Patent protection

A patent gives the owner of an invention the right to take legal action against anyone trying to take commercial advantage without his or her permission. There are four main requirements for something to be regarded as an invention to be covered by patent protection: it must be new; involve an inventive step; be capable of industrial application; and not be excluded by law. Scientific or mathematical theories and mental processes are included in the long list of unpatentable items. Ideas that may encourage offensive, immoral or anti-social behaviour are also excluded.

Obviously it is important to establish first whether or not an idea is really new. A search of patents granted and applied for will give some idea of the activity in the area concerned. This can be done by studying abstracts of published specifications. These are classified under 400 main headings, with 6,000 'catch' words to guide you. Details of classification key are available free of charge from the Patent Office.

For further information contact:

The Chartered Institute of Patent Agents
Staple Inn Buildings
High Holborn
London WC1V 7PZ
Tel: 01 405 9450

The Patent Office
State House
66–71 High Holborn
London WC1R 4TP
Tel: 01 831 2525

Open to the public
Monday–Friday, 1000–1600

The Patent Office produces some free pamphlets covering the field.

Registering designs

The shape, design or decorative features of a commercial product may be protectable by registering the design. The law excludes any shape or appearance which is dictated solely by the production function. Thus, to be registrable a design must be new or original, never published before or, if already known, never applied to the type of product you have in mind. It must also be registered before anyone is shown the design, except in the strictest confidence.

Unlike patent searches, which individuals can do themselves, you must entrust design application work to the officials at the Design Registry.

For further details contact:

The Design Registry,
State House
High Holborn
London WC1R 4TP
Tel: 01 831 2525

Copyright

The copyright laws protect you from the unlicensed copying of 'original' creative works and thus from another company exploiting an inferior copy. Some skill and judgement are required to qualify a work for protection, but the 'originality' itself may be of quite a low order.

The categories protected by copyright include literary works (including not just the obvious, but such items as rules for games, catalogues, advertising copy, etc.); dramatic and musical works; artistic works, including maps, graphs, photographs; films; TV and radio programmes; records, tapes and so on. Computer programs of sufficiently high standard and quality also have protection under copyright law. Copyright is owned by the originator of the program and protection extends to adaptations, conversions into or out of computer language or code and the storage of the program. Video games are also considered to be 'works of art' and if they contain drawings, images, sounds and animation recorded in writing, they are protected under the copyright, Designs and Patents Act 1988.

While the work remains unpublished no legal steps need to be taken to protect it. Once it is published, all you need to do is to add a copyright line to each copy of the work.

It is generally illegal to reproduce copyright work, but less than a substantial part may be used without infringement. The use of the word 'substantial' is more likely to mean important rather than large, though it is up to the courts to interpret.

Trade marks

A trade mark is a symbol by which the goods of a particular manufacturer, merchant or trader can be identified by customers. This can take the form of a word, a signature, a monogram, a picture or logo – or any combination of these. If an unregistered trade mark has been used so extensively that it is clearly associated in customers' minds with a particular brand or product, the users may have acquired a 'reputation' in that mark, which gives them rights under common law.

Otherwise, the process of registration is similar to that of patents. First, a search must be carried out either in person or by a trade mark agent acting for you. Then, using forms from the Trade Marks Registry, you can apply for registration. Once your application has been accepted by the Registry it is advertised in the weekly *Trade Marks Journal*. If this raises no objections the mark is officially registered. Once your mark is registered you have the right to bring an 'infringement' action if anyone else uses your trade mark. The courts also recognize that a trade mark acts as a protection to your customers. When they ask for a branded product by its trade, they can be confident of getting your product and not a 'pirate' product.

For further information contact:

The Institute of Trade Mark Agents
4th Floor, Canterbury House
2–6 Sydenham Road
Croydon CR0 9XE
Tel: 01 686 2052

The Patent Office (whose address is given earlier in this section) also houses the Registrar of Trademarks, who can supply a free pamphlet on the subject:

Registrar of Trademarks Tel: 01 829 6166

Periods of protection

Patents

A patent lasts for twenty years from the date on which you first hand over documents to the Patent Office. After four years from the date you applied for the patent you must pay a yearly fee to keep it effective. Do note, however, that the patent is not fully effective until the specification is published.

Copyright

Copyright in 'artistic' works currently can last for the life of the creator plus fifty years. Copyright on industrial designs lasts only for fifteen years after the product is first marketed.

Registered designs

Registered designs are not protected until registration is complete and then lasts for five years from the date of the application. It can be extended, on payment of a fee, for two additional five-year periods.

D. TRADING LAWS

These areas of law are based on contract law, which is concerned with agreements between willing parties, who exchange promises. Only the parties to a contract are liable for breach of contract. Every business has certain obligations to its customers. These are contained in a number of Acts of Parliament, some of the most important of which are outlined below.

Sale of Goods Act 1979

This Act states that the seller has three obligations.

1. The goods sold must be of merchantable quality – that is, reasonably fit for their normal purpose.
2. The goods must also be fit for any particular purpose made known to the seller. This makes a business responsible for the advice it gives, if, for example, a customer asks whether or not a product will perform a particular job.
3. The goods sold must be as described. This would include the colour or size of the goods concerned.

Consumer Credit Act 1974

This Act covers every aspect of a trader's relationships with customers who buy on credit.

More information is available from:
Consumer Credit Trade Association
Tennyson House
159–163 Great Portland Street
London W1N 5FD
Tel: 01 636 7564

The Food and Drugs Act 1955

This Act makes it a criminal offence to sell unfit food, to describe food falsely or to mislead people about its nature, substance or quality. This regulation covers food wherever it is sold, manufactured, packed, processed or stored for sale.

Prices Act 1974

The Prices Act enables the government to require prices to be displayed and to control the way in which they are displayed. This requires restaurants, pubs, cafés and petrol stations to display their prices.

Trade Descriptions Acts 1968 and 1972

These Acts make it a criminal offence for a trader to describe his or her goods falsely, or to supply goods to which a false description has been applied. The Acts cover such areas as declared car mileage on second-hand cars and statements of the country of manufacture on jeans. They apply to any statement, including the spoken word and advertisements.

Unsolicited Goods and Services Act 1971

The Act makes it an offence to send goods without a customer's order, in the hope that he or she will buy them.

Weights and Measures Acts 1963 and 1979

The Acts make it an offence not to mark the quantity (weight, volume or, in a few cases, the number) on the contents of most packaged grocery items and many other items.

Unfair Contract Terms Act 1977

The Act prevents firms from escaping from their responsibilities by using 'exclusion clauses' or disclaimers, such as statements saying 'articles left at owner's risk'. The onus is on the trader to prove that his or her exclusions are fair and reasonable in the circumstances. The notice itself is not enough.

Consumer Protection Act 1987

This Act safeguards consumers from products that do not reach a reasonable level of safety. Before this Act those injured had to prove a manufacturer negligent before they could successfully sue for damages. While a customer could already sue a supplier without proof of negligence, under the Sale of Goods Act, this Act provides the same rights to anyone injured by a defective product whether or not he or she was the actual buyer.

This Act provides an incentive, where previously it did not exist, for businesses to ensure that their products provide the safety that users, or those affected, can reasonably expect.

For manufacturers, the UK national standard for quality assurance systems laid down in BS 5750 is now compulsory reading.

Data Protection Act 1984

If you have a computer system you must comply with the requirements of this Act. If you hold personal data on individuals in computer files you will need to register as a 'data user' with The Data Protection Registrar. Failure to do so renders you liable to prosecution and, since it can be a criminal offence, may involve imprisonment for offenders. You can obtain further information and forms from the Post Office. There is a simplified registration form for small businesses.

Individuals are entitled to see the information held on them within forty days of having requested it and paid the fee.

Some areas, such as payroll information, material relating to sales and financial information which is kept for your auditors, are exempt.

For more information and advice contact:

Office of the Data Protection Registrar
Springfield House
Water Lane
Wilmslow
Cheshire SK9 5AX
Tel: 0625 535711/535777

Laws covering special trades

Restaurants and all places serving food, employment and nursing agencies, pet shops, taxis, cinemas, betting shops and auction sale rooms are among the hundred or so special trades that have separate additional regulations or licensing requirements.

Your local authority planning department and/or the environmental health department will be able to advise on the regulations that apply specifically to your particular trade.

Open hours

Sunday trading and opening hours may be the subject of local restrictions. Unless you obtain special permission you can offer for sale only a selected variety of merchandise. Once again, a local authority planning department will be able to advise whether or not special local rules apply.

Advertising signs

There are some restrictions on the size and form that the name or advertising hoarding of your premises can take. A look around the neighbourhood will give you an idea of what is acceptable. Before you spend a lot of money, take advice from either the local authority planning department and/or the Department of the Environment. The latter may be contacted at:

Department of the Environment
2 Marsham Street
London SW1P 3EB
Tel: 01 276 3000

E. INSURANCE

Although insurance forms a guarantee against loss, its cost is an overhead, producing no benefit until a calamity occurs. It is therefore a commercial decision as to how much to carry, and it is tempting to minimize cover. The law requires you to carry certain cover, however, as will some contracted obligations, such as those imposed by a mortgage for example.

You should establish your needs by discussing your business plans with an insurance broker or agent, specializing in the appropriate field. Make sure you know exactly what insurance you are buying; and, as insurance is a competitive business, obtain at least three quotations before making up your mind.

Compulsory insurances

Employer's liability

Under the terms of the Employer's Liability (Compulsory Insurance) Act 1969, your business must carry cover to meet your legal liabilities for death or bodily injury suffered by any employee during the course of business. In practice this cover is usually unlimited, with the premiums directly related to your wages bill. The certificate of insurance must be displayed on the premises in a prominent position.

Motor insurance

Private use insurance cover is unlikely to be satisfactory once a businessman or woman starts to use the vehicle for business purposes. That and any other vehicles used in the business should be covered by a 'commercial use' policy. Failure to inform the insurance company may mean that it will not pay out if you or an employee have an accident.

Insurance needed by contracts

Check all the contracts you have to see what insurance you are committed to carry.

Engineering equipment

Certain equipment, such as pressure vessels and lifting tackle, has to be inspected and passed as safe at regular intervals. You can combine maintenance of the equipment with cover against the risk of accidental damage, breakdown, etc.

Other insurance

Personal accident and/or sickness insurance

Employer's liability covers only those accidents in which you, the employer, are held to be legally responsible. You should consider extending that cover to anyone carrying out an especially hazardous task. You may also have to cover your own financial security, particularly if the business depends on your being fit. You may also consider providing an employee scheme for accident or sickness cover as a 'fringe benefit'.

Public liability and product liability

This will protect you against legal liability for death or injury to or damage to the property of a third party on your property. These events can occur through defects in your premises, negligent acts by your employees or from liabilities arising from the product that you market. You need to ensure that the amount of cover is high enough. You may not need product liability insurance if your products are very unlikely to cause any damage or if you are in a service business.

Professional liability

Solicitors, doctors, accountants and management and computer consultants are obvious examples of people involved in giving professional advice. If you are in this sort of business you should consider covering yourself against possible liability arising from wrongful advice and negligence to your clients. This type of claim has been on the increase in recent years, and insurance merits serious consideration.

Business premises, plant and equipment

Quite apart from the legal requirements, these items obviously need cover. There are, however, a number of ways of covering them. 'Reinstatement' provides for full replacement cost, while 'indemnity' meets only the current market value of your asset, which means deducting depreciation first. Other things must also be considered: removal of debris, architect's fees, employees' effects and (potentially the most expensive of all) local authorities sometimes insist that replacement buildings must meet much higher standards than those they replace.

Stock

From raw materials through to finished goods your stock is as exposed as your buildings and plant in the event of fire or another hazard. Since 1982 theft from commercial property has exceeded £50 million a year. Deterioration of stock can also be covered.

Consequential loss

Insurance for consequential loss is intended to restore a business's finances to the position they would have been in had the interruption not occurred. Meeting the replacement costs of buildings, plant, equipment and stock will not compensate for the loss of business and profits arising out of a fire or other disaster. Overheads, employee's wages, etc., may have to continue during the period of interruption. Additional expenses, such as subcontracting work, may also be incurred.

In most cases this insurance is worth taking out - however, if you could easily find somewhere to work, your home perhaps, you may not think it necessary. You may also consider insuring for the cost of finding somewhere else to carry on working rather than insure for the full loss of profits.

Goods in transit

Until your goods reach your customers and are accepted by them, they are still at your risk. You may need to protect yourself from loss or damage in transit. You may not need this cover if you don't sell in this way.

Fidelity guarantee and other thefts

Once in business, thefts can be expected from within and without. A fidelity guarantee can be taken out to gain protection from fraud or dishonesty on the part of key employees. Normal theft cover can be arranged to protect business premises and their contents. It is worth obtaining cover against theft particularly where opportunity is a big factor.

Loss of money

Cash, cheques, stamps, etc., can be insured against theft whether from your premises or in transit. If your takings are in cash this is worth considering.

Credit insurance

This protects you against your customers failing to pay, and you are unlikely to be able to secure this until you have been trading for some time. If you deal in cash or payment on delivery you will probably not need this cover.

You should first consider how much of a problem bad debts are going to be and take advice on setting up a good credit control system. If, however, you have only a few large customers you should consider this insurance in the context of the possibility of failure to pay.

Keyman insurance

More and more businesses are taking out cover on essential members of staff. If your business is dependent on one or two people for its success you can insure against their death. The cash is paid direct to the business.

For further information on insurance matters contact:

The British Insurance and
Investment Brokers Association
BIIBA House
14 Bevis Marks
London EC3A 7NT
Tel: 01 623 9043

BIIBA brokers will take a detailed look at a business, see what risks it is running, and put together a package of policies from different insurers to meet exactly the needs of a client.

For queries about insurance claims contact:

Insurance Ombudsman Bureau,
31 Southampton Row
London WC1B 5HJ
Tel: 01 242 8613

F. EMPLOYING PEOPLE

As soon as you take on your first employee, apart from members of the family, you have to comply with the provisions of the Employment Protection (Consolidation) Act 1978 and associated legislation. Employment law is studded with fines and penalties which can prove expensive for those who, however unwittingly, contravene its practices. Many employers labour under the popular illusion that you cannot sack anyone and that you can barely decide for yourself whom you wish to employ. This is not true. Employment law exists as much to protect the employer as the employee. What it does demand, quite rightly, is that things are done in a fair and reasonable way. The best way to deal with your legal obligations is to spend some time finding out about employment law and then *follow the rules*. In this instance a little planning could save you a great deal of time and money.

Table 7.1 shows at a glance the period of time an employee must be in your service to qualify for various rights, and how entitlement varies according to the number of hours worked per week. The remainder of this chapter summarizes the main legal implications of recruiting and employing people. It is not exhaustive, nor does it cover the complicated minefield of employee relations. Many personnel practitioners keep a reference book handy, one of the best being *Croner's Reference Book for the Self Employed and Smaller Business*. Details of this and other useful publications are given at the end of this chapter with a list of contact addresses.

Table 7.1 Entitlement to employee rights

Employee rights	Length of service required for employees working (hours per week) less than 8	8–16	over 16
1. Discrimination – sex or marital	✓	✓	✓
2. Discriminiation – race	✓	✓	✓
3. Union membership	✓	✓	✓
4. Statement of terms of employment	✗	✗	within 13 weeks of start date
5. Time off – public duties	✗	✗	✓
6. Pay statement	✗	✗	✓
7. Time off – trade union work	✗	✗	✓
8. Time off – trade union activities	✗	✗	✓
9. Time off – safety officer	✗	✗	✓
10. Minimum notice period (1 week)	✗	after 5 years	after 1 month
11. Guarantee payment	✗	after 5 years	after 1 month
12. Pay during suspension on medical grounds	✗	after 5 years	after 1 month
13. Unfair dismissal – statement of reasons	after 6 months	after 6 months	after 6 months
14. Maternity pay:			
Lower rate	✗	after 5 years	after 26 weeks
Higher rate	✗	after 5 years	after 2 years
15. Maternity leave – right to return	✗	after 5 years	after 2 years
16. Redundancy payment	after 2 years	after 2 years	after 2 years

Young people

Provisions laid down in the Young Persons (Employment) Acts 1938 and 1964 regulate the hours and age of employment for young people – those of either sex over the compulsory school age (currently sixteen) but not yet eighteen – in certain circumstances. The Department of Employment produces a leaflet giving the information you will need to check (see Section J: Sources of information).

Retired people

In certain circumstances you can employ individuals who have reached the state retirement age. They may lose certain protection rights laid down in the Employment Protection (Consolidation) Act 1978 and employers will still be liable for secondary national insurance contributions.

Disabled people

If you employ more than twenty people, under the provisions of the Disabled Persons (Employment) Acts 1944 and 1958 you must ensure that a quota of 3 per cent of your workforce are registered disabled people. Some industries and types of particularly dangerous work are exempt but you must check with the Department of Employment. You can refuse to employ someone if you are unhappy about the state of his or her health but you should ask for a medical check if you take this course.

Criminal offences

You cannot technically deny employment on the grounds that an individual was once convicted although the courts cannot compel you to employ ex-offenders.

Some convictions leading to imprisonment are 'spent' after seven years and do not have to be disclosed on a job application form or at an interview. If you subsequently discover the truth you cannot fairly dismiss the individual. Other convictions leading to a sentence of longer than two and a half years in prison are never 'spent' and should be declared.

If you have problems in this area you should refer to the Rehabilitation of Offenders Act 1974.

Discrimination

Broadly speaking, you must not discriminate on the grounds of sex, race or marital status and you must not refuse permission for your employees to join a trade union or dismiss them for trade union activity. Discrimination means less favourable treatment of one individual than another. Among other things it covers pay, conditions of work, promotion and training. You cannot discriminate in any of the following circumstances:

(a) advertising or interviewing for a job;
(b) terms of employment;
(c) selection procedures;
(d) promotion, transfer and training;

(e) benefits offered to workers;
(f) dismissals.

You should take particular care not to make it more difficult for one group of people to meet requirements, for example for promotion, than another. Insisting that a person must be six feet tall would preclude most women, and would be seen as discrimination.

If you can show, however, that particular requirements are necessary to do the job effectively, the case would be allowable. You should remember too that the Sex Discrimination Act covers both men and women and either sex can make a complaint.

Employees can also complain to a tribunal if you penalize or dismiss them for trying to join, or joining, an independent trade union - you can check with the Certification Office if you are unsure about the status of a trade union. You must allow employees to take part in activities, such as meetings, connected with the union either outside or, by agreement with you, inside working hours. Industrial action is not recognized as union activity but your employees can picket in small numbers if they are in dispute with you.

Codes of practice are available giving guidelines for the elimination of discrimination and conduct and procedures covering many aspects of employee relations. Before taking any action which will entangle you in trade union law or discrimination proceedings, take advice; the solution can often be simpler than it may at first seem.

Contact address is:

The Certification Office for
Trades Unions and Employers' Associations
27 Wilton Street
London SW1X 7AZ
Tel: 01 210 3734

Contracts of employment

A full contract of employment can be oral or written and may be the result of extended negotiation or casual conversation. Terms of the contract can be varied only by agreement, such agreement being expressed or implied by the individual concerned or from the terms of your collective bargaining with a trade union.

The contract exists as soon as the individual agrees to start work, and becomes effective when terms and conditions have been agreed. Be warned: 'promises' made at an interview, or in subsequent conversations, which are not later offered are deemed part of the contract and by not fulfilling them you will be 'in breach' of the contract.

The contract should cover all aspects of a person's employment including wages (bonuses and commission), overtime payments, sick pay, travel allowances, pensions, holidays (including public holidays) and holiday pay (including how it is calculated), hours of work, period of notice (on both sides) and a statement of information about disciplinary and grievance procedures. You also have to state whether you have a contracting-out certificate under the Social Security Pensions Act 1975 as it applies to the employee.

The written statement of employment

An employee who works over sixteen hours per week, or has worked over eight hours per week for five years, is entitled to receive a written statement of employment within thirteen weeks of starting the job or qualifying for the entitlement. This statement must cover:

(a) employer's name;
(b) job title;
(c) date of employment starting;
(d) pay;
(e) sick pay;
(f) pensions;
(g) hours of work;
(h) holiday entitlement;
(i) length of notice;
(j) disciplinary rules;
(k) grievance procedures.

In many cases the statement forms the bones of the full contract and at the same time satisfies your legal obligations.

G. PAYING PEOPLE

Wages

'Wages' includes any forms of pay stated in the contract of employment and others which are covered by statute, for example maternity pay. It does not include expenses, redundancy payments, pension allowances/payments, 'golden handshakes' or compensation for loss of office.

In most cases how much and how often you pay will be decided between you and your employee. The Wages Act 1986 applies to all your employees and is the formal expression of 'a fair day's pay for a fair day's work'. Some industries – including some retail, some catering, hairdressing, clothing manufacturers and laundries – have terms regulated by a Wages Council. If you do not pay the established minimum hourly and overtime rates or provide minimum holiday entitlement you are liable to be fined. People under twenty-one are not covered by Wages Council provisions.

Equal pay

The Equal Pay Act 1970 requires that you pay equal amounts to men and women engaged on 'like work' (same job) or 'work of equal value' (equivalent work in terms of effort, skill, decision-making). Complaints about pay are referred to the Industrial Tribunal.

Deductions

By law you must deduct tax from pay at source (PAYE) for all employees. Your local tax office will advise you on amounts and provide tax codes. You must also deduct national insurance contributions for yourself and for each employee. The Department of Health and Social Security (DHSS) has a useful leaflet giving guidelines for the procedures. You can obtain this from your local office.

You cannot make any other deduction from your employee's pay unless it has been laid down by law or agreed in writing by the employee.

Itemized pay statements

You are obliged to provide an itemized statement of pay, showing gross pay, all deductions, and net pay.

Holiday pay

You do not have to pay employees over their holiday period unless you have agreed to do so or if this condition of employment is regulated by a Wages Council.

Sick pay

There is a legal requirement to pay staff who are sick and who qualify under certain conditions. This is covered by the Statutory Sick Pay (SSP) Scheme, on which you can obtain advice from the DHSS. To receive SSP your employee must provide evidence, usually a certificate, that the illness lasted for more than four consecutive days, including Sundays and public holidays. The rules governing SSP are complicated and it would help to have a copy of the DHSS leaflet available.

Maternity arrangements

If a woman meets the qualifying conditions, as shown in Table 7.1, she is normally entitled to:

(a) 90 per cent of normal pay for the first six weeks of her absence – minus the flat-rate maternity allowance, which can be claimed back from the Maternity Fund;
(b) return to her job, or a suitable alternative, provided she gives notice of her intention before her absence and confirms this in writing twenty-one days before her return.

The job must be held open for up to twenty-nine weeks following the woman's confinement (date of baby's birth) if she wishes to return.

Although the onus is on the employee to comply with the rules, you should make sure that your staff are aware of the maternity arrangements. This is usually done by inclusion in the contract of employment.

If you employ less than five people, you can legitimately claim that it is not possible to take back the employee.

Time off work

Employees do have rights to take, paid or unpaid, reasonable time off work for certain, specified reasons. These are:

(a) for ante-natal appointments (paid);
(b) to look for work (two years' service required – paid);
(c) for public duties (e.g. magistrates – sometimes paid);
(d) to attend safety training courses (paid – safety representatives only);
(e) to carry out trade union duties, where a trade union is recognized (unpaid – but paid for union officials).

H. HEALTH AND SAFETY AT WORK

This aspect of employing people is covered by the Health and Safety at Work etc. Act 1974. Inspectors have wide powers to implement this legislation and failure to comply can result not only in fines but imprisonment. You are obliged to provide a reasonable standard of health and safety to employees and visitors, whether members of the public or workers, and to ensure the safety of anyone who may be affected by what you do. This applies to your premises and any risk involved in the work itself.

Once you have employees you must contact your local authority or your Health and Safety Executive area office to inform them of your business name and address. You must obtain employer's liability insurance and display your latest certificate for employees to see. If you employ more than five people you must also have a written policy statement of the firm's commitment to health and safety, specifying how you intend to ensure that this commitment is met in practice. All employees must receive a copy. If you have ten or more employees you must keep an accident book to record work accidents. This procedure is compulsory for factory owners regardless of the number of employees.

Making your premises safe includes looking at things like fire exits, extinguishers, electrical fittings, storing materials, machinery, hygiene and first aid. The list is very long and covers all aspects of work. An inspector has the right to enter your workplace and examine it.

The Health and Safety Executive produces a number of useful booklets which will help you with the essentials. There is also a catalogue listing more than 2,000 relevant publications covering this area or legislation available from HMSO (see Section J: Sources of information).

I. DISMISSAL

The unfair dismissal provisions contained in the Employment Protection (Consolidation) Act 1978 apply to anyone qualifying for the entitlement, as shown in Table 7.1. You have two years to assess an individual, during which time you can dismiss him or her without fear of an unfair dismissal accusation, unless it is a charge of discrimination.

Broadly speaking, the law demands that you behave in a fair and reasonable way when dismissing an employee and in strict conformity with the relevant code. An individual who feels that his or her dismissal was based on unfair reasons might qualify to take the case to an Industrial Tribunal. If the claim is upheld you will be liable for damages or to reinstate the individual. However, the law cannot make you re-employ someone once he or she has been dismissed. Fair dismissal can be based only on one of the following:

(a) the capabilities/qualifications of the employee, provided that the contract states that the job requires them;
(b) employee's conduct;
(c) redundancy;
(d) if the employee would be breaking the law were he or she to continue in the job;
(e) some other justified, substantial reason;
(f) on transfer of the business, in certain circumstances.

The government codes of practice issued under the Employment Protection Act 1975 clearly set out policy and practice for disciplinary and grievance procedures. Although the codes are not legally binding they are designed to indicate acceptable standards and are taken into consideration, with the relevant statute, as a supplement and guide to the law. Tribunals do take into account the size and resources of the firm when deciding whether dismissal is unfair or not. They may consider that your company is too small or under-resourced to be obliged to provide written warnings, a right of appeal or to conduct full-scale investigation without seriously hampering the running of the business.

In the majority of cases tribunals are likely to hold that small firms necessarily expect the highest standards of conduct, and that they should be allowed considerable flexibility to vary contracts of employment. In addition, it may help to know that less than 10 per cent of all unfair dismissal claims actually proceed as far as a hearing and are proven. Compensation amounts are not huge – typically around £1,500 or less – but time spent in preparation far outweighs these 'benefits'. The main point to remember is that you must be able to show that in all circumstances, including the size of the business, you acted fairly and reasonably and you followed the proper procedures.

J. SOURCES OF INFORMATION

Institute of Personnel Management

The Institute has 33,000 individual members, and has extended its service to businesses through its Company Service Plan. Membership is by annual subscription and a one-off entrance fee. This gives access to the Institute's library, publications, conferences and seminars, and, more importantly, it allows use of the Information and Advisory Service, staffed by a small team of multi-disciplinary specialists, including a legal adviser who is a barrister. The Service can answer or find answers to most problems in this field. Inquiries can be made by letter, telephone or personal visit between 0900 and 1700 daily, Monday to Friday.

Interestingly enough, of the 300 or so inquiries handled each month, pay and conditions account for half, followed by employment law, employee relations and then training.

Further information may be obtained from:

Institute of Personnel Management
IPM House
35 Camp Road
Wimbledon
London SW19 4UW
Tel: 01 946 9100

Jobcentres

As well as providing employees, Jobcentres can also advise on most aspects of employment law, or at any rate effect introductions to other local organizations able to help.

Other useful sources of published information

The following list may be helpful:

Advisory Conciliation and Arbitration Service (ACAS)

- Code of Practice 1: Disciplinary and Grievance Procedures
- Code of Practice 2: Collective Bargaining - Information Required
- Code of Practice 3: Time Off - Trade Unions
- Fair and Unfair Dismissal; a Guide for Employers
- Employment legislation booklets
- The Law on Unfair Dismissal - Guidance for Small Firms
- Individual Rights of Employees: A Guide for Employers

Contact:

ACAS Head Office
Clifton House
83–117 Euston Road
London NW1 2RB
Tel: 388 5100

Commission for Racial Equality

- Code of Practice - Racial Discrimination

Contact:

Commission for Racial Equality
Elliot House
10–12 Allington Street
London SW1E 5EH
Tel: 01 828 7022

Confederation of British Industry (CBI)

- Directory of trade associations
- Committee of non-statutory training organizations

Contact:

CBI
Centre Point
New Oxford Street
London WC1A 1DU
Tel: 01 379 7400

Croner Publications

- *Croner's Reference Book for Employers*
- *Croner's Reference Book for the Self-Employed and Smaller Business*

Contact:

Croner Publications Ltd
Croner House
London Road
Kingston upon Thames
Surrey KT2 6SR
Tel: 01 547 3333

Equal Opportunities Commission

- Sex discrimination case law
- Code of Practice: Sex Discrimination
- Equal opportunities policies

Contact:

Equal Opportunities Commission
Overseas House
Quay Street
Manchester M3 3HN
Tel: 061 833 9244

Health and Safety Executive

- Essentials of Health and Safety at Work (available from HMSO).

Contact:

Health and Safety Executive
Baynards House
Chepstow Place
Westbourne Grove
London W2 4TF
Tel: 01 229 3456

Her Majesty's Stationery Office

HMSO holds and sells all government statutes and corresponding advisory leaflets.

Contact:

HMSO
P O Box 276
London SW8 5DT
Inquiries - Tel: 01 873 0011
Orders - Tel: 01 873 9090